WOK THIS WAY

The essential guide to cooking with a wok—with recipes for . . .

- Gingered Beef with Asparagus
- Chicken, Corn, and Red Pepper Stir-Fry
- Mu Shu Pork
- Clams in Black Bean Sauce
- Maple Gingerbread
- Spicy Tofu and Broccoli with Sesame Sauce
- Tex-Mex Stir-Fry
- Simmered Chicken Wings
- Vegetable Stir-Fry

and much, much more!

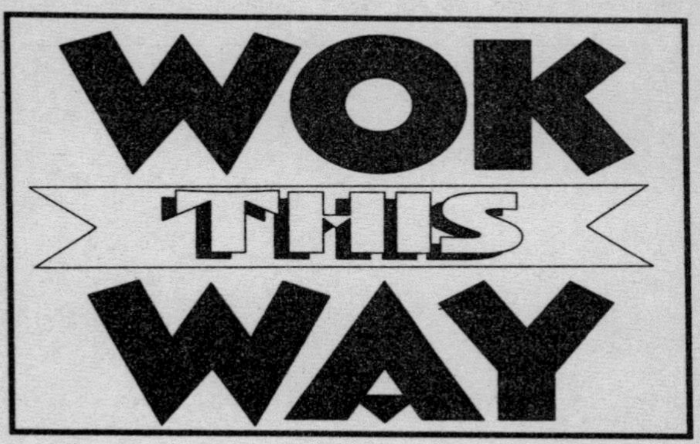

Allison Marx

Produced by The Philip Lief Group, Inc.

Produced by The Philip Lief Group, Inc.

WOK THIS WAY

A Berkley Book / published by arrangement with
The Philip Lief Group, Inc.

PRINTING HISTORY
Berkley edition / April 1994

ISBN: 0-425-14187-X

BERKLEY®
Berkley Books are published by The Berkley Publishing Group,
200 Madison Avenue, New York, New York 10016.
BERKLEY and the "B" design
are trademarks belonging to Berkley Publishing Corporation.

PRINTED IN THE UNITED STATES OF AMERICA

10 9 8 7 6 5 4 3 2 1

CONTENTS

ACKNOWLEDGMENTS

This was the dream and you helped me make it come true:

Lee Ann and Julia for giving me the opportunity.

Karyn Wagner, my mentor and friend.

Joanne Marx, my mom, cooking teacher, and researcher extraordinaire.

Michael Dooley, my husband, my typist and taste-tester, my champion.

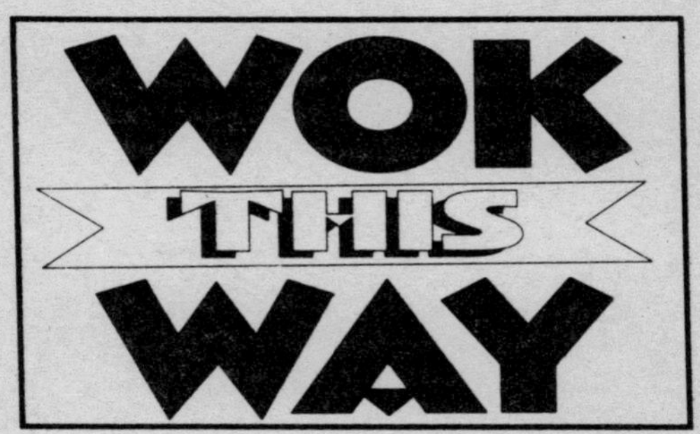
WOK
THIS
WAY

Introduction

Why a wok? People have been using frying pans and saucepans with great success for centuries, so why a wok?

People have been using woks for centuries, too. Woks are the primary cooking pots for Chinese cuisine, and many other Asian cultures use pots that are bowl-shaped like a wok. Woks do double duty as frying and saucepans. In Chinese households an oven is a rarity, so a covered wok becomes a stove-top oven for steamed breads and sweet cakes, simmered stews, and puddings. Woks are big and roomy, so you can stir and toss the food with abandon and not fear that your dinner will end up on the floor. They have sloped sides, so whether you are cooking for two or twelve, the food will gracefully gather at the center of the wok. Best of all, wok cooking is fast, easy, and flavorful. Woks are so versatile and easy to use that you will probably find many more uses for your wok than can be included in this one book.

This book will guide you step-by-step through buying a wok and learning how to use it. The first wok cooking technique we'll discuss is stir-frying; it is also the most well-known use for the wok. Stir-frying is especially popular because many stir-fry recipes meet low-fat guidelines for a healthy diet. These recipes are served with a generous portion of rice and use lots of vegetables, small amounts of meat, poultry, or fish and very little oil. Stir-frying is the best place to start and is so versatile that I have included a chapter of recipes for your stir-fry leftovers. You might try making a double batch of these recipes so you can be sure that you will have some leftovers.

The Chinese cooking techniques used for wok cooking are sound guidelines that can be applied to all types of cooking. These techniques are the foundation for all of the recipes in this book. All wok cooking is based on planning and preparation. Planning, as with all things in life, is the best way to ensure a successful outcome. All the ingredients are peeled, chopped, and ready, all the sauces are mixed, and seasonings are laid out for use before any cooking begins. Restaurants rely on this principle of preparation. Whether the restaurant is Chinese, French, or Mexican, they need to have all the ingredients ready and at hand for cooking. You will find that the cooking itself takes very little time once all the preparation is done.

Wok cooking does take preparation one step further. No knives are needed at the Chinese dining table because the food is already cut into bite-size pieces. Foods are seasoned throughout the cooking process, as opposed to salting and peppering foods after they have come to the table. This allows the flavor of the seasoning to permeate. When you sit down to eat, your only job is to enjoy.

Each dish you prepare will be a combination of flavors, textures, and colors. Combinations of hot and sour, smooth and crunchy, and sweet and salty are common to Chinese cooking. The chapter in this book called "Summer Wok" is about combining cold and hot or room-temperature foods. In each recipe, flavors are contrasted and balanced against one another. Foods of varying colors and textures are combined. A wok-cooked diet utilizes a variety of meat, fish, seasonings, and vegetables. The diet is well-balanced, without too much of any one ingredient, and your palate is tantalized by the play among the different flavors that complement and contrast one another. Learning the flavor combinations that characterize Chinese wok cooking is intriguing.

The flavors we work with in preparing a dish begin and end with the ingredients themselves. Getting foods at the peak of their flavor is primary. Some of the recipes in this book have names like Winter Stir-Fry and Summer Noodles to make it easy for you to know when the ingredients for these dishes will be at their best. It is better to substitute another similar fresh ingredient than to make do with a substandard ingredient, but if this can't be done, you can use many tricks to help you work with what you have. A bit of sugar harmonizes the flavors in a dish and minimizes salty or sharp flavors. A bit of wine helps to bring out the flavor of fish and gives dishes a distinct fragrance. Salt will draw moisture and bitterness out of eggplant and make meats juicier, and a marinade will tenderize a tough cut of meat.

Every day when you are deciding what to make for dinner, you either go to the store to choose sweet, fresh ingredients or you make do with what is in the cupboard. The Chinese of today and centuries ago, and the writer of this book, follow that same path when developing recipes.

Cooking of all cultures progresses under the forces of wealth and poverty. The wealthy hire cooks whose attentions are concentrated on developing new and creative concoctions. Choices are made out of a desire to be creative, to try something new, or to accent the flavor of a particularly tasty morsel. The recipes of the leisure class were developed for art itself, to surprise or impress. The other class of recipes are the recipes of necessity. The poor contribute to culinary history by utilizing the age-old principle that necessity is the mother of invention. Pigs don't require much land and are not as particular about what they eat as cows, so the poor developed more pork dishes. Stir-frying was developed because food cooks quickly, so less fuel is needed to prepare a meal. We now have the best of both worlds, utilizing the cooking techniques developed by the chefs of the rich combined with the ingenuity of the poor.

I have tried to include in this book some of the lessons I have learned—tricks and tidbits that I hope will stay with you when you explore other styles of cooking:

Oil and water don't mix, so foods that are washed should be patted dry for sautéing, stir-frying, or deep frying. Foods are often dredged in flour or cornstarch to give them a dry surface for this reason. The exception is marinades. (I have learned that there is always an exception.)

Use your judgment to decide the size of portions. Most Chinese meals consist of more than one dish. Serve rice with all Oriental dishes that don't contain another starch such as noodles or wontons. I often prepare two contrasting dishes for a meal—a cold dish and a hot dish, or a fish dish and a meat dish, or a mild dish and a spicy dish. Measure out in your mind the amount of meat and vegetables you will be using. Is that enough food, or do you eat more or less than that? Plan accordingly.

Enough talk, let's wok!

PART ONE

WOK COOKING

Choosing a Wok

The old-fashioned, round-bottomed wok that sits on a ring is growing less common every day. A round-bottomed wok heats more evenly, but it is an awkward appliance. It should not be used on electric stoves and, if your house is anything like mine, the ring is just one more thing to misplace. Most woks made today are slightly flat on the bottom so they can sit directly on your stove without a ring.

Cast-iron and carbon steel are the traditional materials for woks. They must be seasoned (instructions on how to season a wok are in the next chapter) and after each use they must be carefully cooked dry to prevent rusting, but they heat up well and are true woks. A carbon steel wok is inexpensive and lightweight. It blackens with age, so it is not for the cook who needs all her appliances to be sparkling and hanging like artwork above the stove. Cast-iron woks are heavy and difficult to maneuver if you have to roll oil around in the wok or shake the wok to move food around. Cast-iron woks do heat well and evenly, though, and add small amounts of iron to your diet.

A nonstick wok is a wok-shaped pan that functions like a wok, but there is a magical quality lacking: The residue of past meals that lives on as your wok blackens with age is missing. However, you use slightly less oil in cooking and there are a few sticky recipes that will come out much better in a nonstick wok.

Anodized aluminum woks are attractive and have a very comfortable weight, but they also aren't quite the same as the classic carbon steel wok. A single-handled anodized aluminum wok and a two-handled carbon steel wok are my two cooking favorites. Cast-iron is too heavy and electric woks don't let you control the heat as immediately as a wok on a gas stove. Electric woks are terrific for cooking such dishes as broth fondue and bananas flambé at the table.

A wok must be big, twelve to sixteen inches in diameter at the top rim. The space is needed whether you are cooking for two or twelve, and a large wok can do both. Several companies have recently come out with small woks, but I do not recommend them.

One final consideration is how you intend to use your wok. If you intend to do a lot of deep-frying, choose a two-handled wok for stability. If you intend to stir-fry, choose a carbon steel wok. If you will be poaching and steaming your dinners, don't choose a carbon steel wok because the seasoned surface that gets cooked on will flake off with frequent poaching. All woks can be used for frying, stir-frying, steaming, and poaching, but each wok has its strengths and weaknesses.

Tools of the Wok

Lid

A lid is important if you wish to steam and stew in your wok. Not all woks come with a lid. If yours has no lid, you can buy one at most cookware stores. The lid should be dome-shaped and its rim should rest inside the rim of the wok and seal the wok well, so steam does not escape during cooking.

Something to Stir With

The Chinese spatula has a curved end that easily follows the curve of the wok and raised sides that catch and hold food like a spoon. The shape of the spatula allows you to lift and flip food easily. Wooden spoons and rubber or metal spatulas can also be used. A flat wooden or plastic spatula is useful if you have a nonstick wok and can't use the Chinese metal spatula. Wooden chopsticks are also good for stirring and terrific for retrieving a single strand of pasta to test for doneness.

Something to Cut With

A cleaver is a versatile knife that can chop through bone as easily as it minces parsley. The wide flat blade is used to carry chopped ingredients to the wok for cooking. Some people, myself included, are not comfortable with the heavy weight of a cleaver. I do use my cleaver for cutting through bones and the long straight blade is terrific for mincing herbs and ginger, but for chopping vegetables I frequently use a smaller, lighter knife that I keep very sharp. It is a matter of personal preference. When I use my smaller knife, I use a metal pastry scraper to carry the vegetables to the wok.

Steamer

If you do much steaming, you will quickly find the need for a tiered bamboo steamer. It triples the amount of space you have for steaming. The steam is absorbed into the bamboo, so less water drips down into the food. It has a snug lid and tends to be more stable than other steaming racks. Many people place heat-safe pans above the water in woks for steaming, or steam on a single round metal rack. These methods work well, but the bamboo variety still gets my vote.

Tools for Deep Frying

A Chinese mesh strainer looks like a chicken-wire ladle. The oil can easily drip through and away from the cooked food. A slotted spoon can be used instead. Use tongs for removing food or moving food around so pieces don't stick to each other. A wok rack often comes with your wok. It is half round and hangs off the edge of the wok. Fried food can be placed on the rack to drain while still staying warm above the hot oil.

Something to Clean Your Wok With

A bamboo brush is ideal, but plastic scrubbers or even a loofah sponge can do the job. Never use steel wool on a wok.

Rice Serving Spoon

You don't need one, but I enjoy and use mine so much that I thought you might like to know about it. It is a large round spoon (not oval, like most spoons) with a short wooden handle. It's perfect for serving rice, but is also great for scooping up other dishes you cook in the wok. The short wooden handle makes it the right size and look for use at the table.

One More Pot

I have tried to create recipes that don't require any other equipment. You don't need a microwave or a blender for most of the recipes, but you will need one more pot: a good-sized saucepan with a lid for cooking rice and noodles.

Bowls

I couldn't get by without my bowls. I mix all the sauces, toss meat with marinades, and hold all the vegetables that have to be chopped and set aside in steep-sided Chinese rice bowls. These glazed ceramic bowls are nonreactive with marinades. Soup bowls, pasta bowls, and tea cups are all useful and are a better size than traditional mixing bowls, and they will work just as well.

Ingredients

In every cuisine there are ordinary elements and exotic elements. The simplest and most common ingredients can be combined to make wonderful and delicious new dishes, without your ever needing to hunt down spices you can't even pronounce. Many of the dishes in this book contain ingredients you can easily find in your supermarket.

On the other hand, some cooks love the hunt. They treasure the chance to understand how to cook with Chinese black beans, or to try Chinese sausages. I must admit to being a cook who lives for the exotic. Chinese five-spice powder can be found in the Chinese food section of most supermarkets. Some will walk by it and never even know it's there and some will stop and pick up a bottle. They'll head home not even knowing what it is they have purchased, but determined to discover its secrets. I hope you will indulge me when I offer you a recipe that seeks to release the magic powers of the exotic on unsuspecting chicken breasts or an innocent eggplant.

Here is a list of the ingredients used in Chinese wok cooking. I have tried to list substitutions for certain ingredients that are difficult to find, and recipes for sauces that are available bottled, but that you might like to try making at home. I also mention even more exotic ingredients that you might want to experiment with.

Salted Black Beans (also Called Fermented Black Beans)

The beans are rinsed or soaked before using, and are only used in small quantities for black bean sauce. They are actually soybeans that have been fermented in brine. Their salty flavor is especially terrific with fish and they are often used in conjunction with garlic.

Chinese Parsley (also Called Cilantro, Fresh Coriander, or Fragrant Green)

This is one of the very few herbs used in Chinese cookery. It looks much like parsley but has a distinct fragrance and sharp flavor that is very different. Chinese parsley is sold with the roots still attached to distinguish it from regular parsley. To store cilantro, set the roots in a cup of water and place it in the refrigerator.

Citrus

Used to make dishes such as Lemon Chicken and Chicken with Orange Sauce, citrus is a treasured flavor in wok cooking. Fresh oranges are the most common dessert for a Chinese meal. Dried orange and tangerine peel concentrates the flavor and can be purchased dried or easily dried at home.

Cornstarch

Cornstarch is not a seasoning, but it is used with seasonings to thicken sauces. Cornstarch is combined with a bit of water to form a thin paste and then mixed with seasonings such as soy sauce or wine. These sauces are added at the end of stir-frying. If you learn only one thing from this book, let that be how to make and use cornstarch paste to thicken sauces to an appealing texture with a shiny glaze.

Five-Spice Powder

A fragrant and full-flavored combination of spices usually used in combination with soy sauce, five-spice powder contains cinnamon, star anise and/or anise seeds, cloves, fennel seeds, and Szechuan peppercorns. If you want to make your own, see the recipe on page 36.

Garlic

Use garlic minced, sliced, or whole in recipes. When used whole or cut in half, the clove can be removed before the dish is served. When sliced, the garlic is usually slowly sautéed at a lower temperature than stir-frying. I estimate that an average-size garlic clove is about a teaspoon worth of minced garlic, but garlic cloves do come in a wide variety of sizes, so it is only an estimate. Garlic is added to the oil in a stir-fry at the very beginning of cooking so that it flavors the oil. A few garlic tricks: garlic cloves stored in water will peel easily, and smashing a garlic clove under the blade of a cleaver makes for lickety-split mincing.

Ginger

Ginger is a root and looks it; it is gnarled and light brown. In spring the roots are young and tender and can be used more generously at that time of year. Ginger is used minced or in slices. If you would like to add ginger flavor to a dish and not add the root itself, then put slices through a garlic press and reserve the juice. When a slice is called for, use a slice the thickness and diameter of a quarter. Cut off and discard the end slice of a ginger root if it is dried up. Ginger should be kept wrapped and refrigerated. When ginger is needed in a recipe, use fresh ginger; powdered ginger is for baking and should not be substituted for fresh ginger.

Hoisin Sauce
This thick sauce made from soy, vinegar, sugar, garlic, and spices is both spicy and sweet and is used to season dishes, or as a condiment dipping sauce.

Hot Spices
When used judiciously, hot spices add flavor to dishes. It is not our intention to create any dish that is too hot to eat, so use these spices sparingly; you can always add more. The heat of chilies is in the seeds. If you wish to cook with whole chilies, remove the seeds; the pulp is plenty hot. I do not leave chilies in food for some unsuspecting guest to bite into. Following are common hot spices used in the recipes in this book:

Red Pepper Flakes: The dried seeds of hot peppers.
Tabasco Brand Hot Sauce: I believe it has the best flavor of all the hot pepper sauces.
Szechuan Chili Peppers: Very hot small red peppers.
Chili Oil: This oil is a seasoning. It is made from oil and small, red Szechuan chili peppers. It is usually quite hot, so use it sparingly.

Oil
Peanut oil is considered the best for stir-frying and deep-frying because it smokes and burns less easily than other oils, but any light-flavored oil will suffice. Corn oil or safflower oil are acceptable alternatives. Do not use butter or margarine to stir-fry as they burn much too easily.

Oyster Sauce
A thick, smooth, dark sauce of soy and oysters, the taste is not fishy and it enhances the flavor of many dishes, most

commonly beef. (See our recipe for Oyster Sauce on page 37.)

Plum Sauce

Plum sauce is a variety of duck sauce. Both are thick chutney sauces that combine fruit with vinegar, sugar, and a bit of chili. Duck sauce uses apricots, and plum sauce, obviously, uses plums. It goes well with roasted meats and fried dishes. A spicy sweet fruit condiment called chutney can be used as a substitute. For Mu Shu, combine two parts plum sauce with one part Hoisin sauce.

Sesame Oil

Buy the dark variety of sesame oil for our recipes. The bottle may not indicate that it's dark sesame oil, so you must differentiate it from regular sesame oil by its color. Sesame oil is used as a seasoning due to its flavor and aroma, and it should not be used as cooking oil. Often it is added just at the end of the cooking process.

Soy Sauce

A thin, salty sauce of fermented soy beans, water, and flour. Light soy sauce is the most common kind. When a recipe calls for soy sauce, it is referring to the light variety. There are several other varieties of soy sauce that are darker or thicker than the regular soy sauce. They are used in slow-cooked meat dishes and as dipping sauces for fried foods. Those who like the exotic should try mushroom soy sauce. Use it in dishes that contain mushrooms. If you have the chance to visit a Chinese grocery, splurge on a bottle of good-quality aged soy sauce; the flavor is rich and savory. Dark soy sauce is thicker and sweeter. To use dark soy sauce, replace half the amount of soy sauce called for in the recipe with dark soy sauce for a richer flavor.

Stock

Stock can be used to make soups, to flavor steamed foods, and it is reduced to make sauces. Broth or stock is also wonderful for serving as a separate course before or after a meal. It isn't necessarily made in a wok, but it is useful for your wok cooking. Stock is wonderfully flavorful and nutritious. Using a stock to make a sauce or to steam food is a natural flavor enhancer. Use fish stock when steaming fish, or chicken stock instead of water to make a richer sauce for a stir-fry. You can also buy broth in cans if you can't or don't want to make your own.

Meat and poultry stocks do take a bit of time, but not very much work. I always make a gallon at a time and then I don't have to make stock all that often. The primary ingredient for stock is bones. You can save bones from meals you serve and freeze them until you have enough to make a whole pot of stock, or you can go to your butcher for bones. Often butchers will give a regular customer bones free of charge.

Seasoning for a stock should be kept simple so as not to conflict with the seasoning choices of a recipe. After the stock is cooked and strained, divide it into small containers for freezing. Ice cubes of stock defrost quickly and can be used when only a small amount of stock is needed.

Sweeteners

A sweetener, often sugar, is used in very small quantities in many recipes to cover unpleasant flavors, highlight pleasant ones, and bring together the salty and spicy flavors in Chinese sauces. Different sweeteners have different flavors. Brown sugar is mellower than white sugar, and honey has a totally different flavor. The sweetness of the type of sugar should be considered, but also take into account the flavor of the sweetener. Try experimenting with rice syrup or malt sugar (available at health food stores). The quantities of sugar used are so small that the calorie count is negligible, so do not use sugar substitutes. Substitutes do not have the flavor or harmonizing qualities that real sweeteners do.

Szechuan Peppercorns

They look like peppercorns that have popped. They are actually not a type of pepper, but a dried berry. Szechuan peppercorns have a bit of spicy flavor. When roasted lightly in a dry wok with kosher or sea salt, the peppercorns make a tasty dip for fried foods.

Teriyaki Sauce

A sweet soy sauce marinade, teriyaki sauce is often used for grilling meat, fish, and poultry. It's also a good dipping sauce for fried foods.

Vinegar

Rice wine vinegar comes seasoned and unseasoned. When vinegar is called for in this book, you should use the unseasoned variety. The seasoned kind has salt and sugar added to it. Cider, white vinegar, and white wine vinegar can be substituted for rice wine vinegar, but do not substitute red wine vinegar. Red and black rice wine vinegar are rare Chinese vinegars and are used as condiments. They are not used in recipes in this book but are fun to try with dumplings and fried foods.

Wines

I do not recommend cooking with anything that is labeled "cooking wine." Sherry, which is used in many recipes, is good because it is fragrant and full-bodied. The sherry you choose should be dry. Rice wine is the traditional wine used in Chinese cooking and is interchangeable with sherry in most recipes. I have used sherry in most of the recipes in this book because it is also used in many non-Chinese recipes, so people tend to have it around. It is easier to find than rice wine, but try both and decide for yourself. Most white wine does not have as much flavor, texture, or aroma as rice wine or sherry, but if you prefer a milder taste, then white wine may be substituted.

Foods You Can Prepare in a Wok:

Baby Corn

Available in cans, baby corn is tender and sweet. It should be rinsed well before using. The entire ear, cob and all, is edible and does not need to be cooked. Cook only to heat through.

Bamboo Shoots

The tender shoots of a bamboo plant are available canned in water. Rinse before using and store immersed in water. Bamboo shoots are a tiny bit fibrous, pale in color, with a touch of crunch.

Bean Curd or Tofu

Made from soybeans, the way cheese and custard are made from milk, tofu is high in protein and low in fat and is available soft or firm. The difference between the two textures is the amount of water they contain. Soft is best for soups, and firm is preferred for stir-fried dishes. Bean curd has little flavor of its own, but it absorbs the flavor of sauces it is cooked with.

Bean Sprouts

Sprouted from the mung bean, bean sprouts are long, thin, and white. They are crunchy and are often used to garnish dishes.

Bok Choy

A leafy green-and-white vegetable. The stems are white and the leafy tips are green. The leaves taste like Swiss chard or mustard greens and the stems taste similar to celery.

Chinese Broccoli

Much like broccoli rabe, it has more stem and leaves, and less florets than regular broccoli.

Chinese or Napa Cabbage

Chinese cabbage is a long rather than round cabbage. The ends of the leaves are frilly and almost as light as lettuce. It is a lighter cabbage than our round-headed cabbage. To substitute, use a combination of standard cabbage and lettuce.

Chinese Preserved Vegetables

These are mustard greens soaked in brine, then fermented. Rinse well before using.

Chicken and Other Poultry

Boneless chicken breasts are often called for in stir-fry recipes. A boneless chicken breast is a butterfly-shaped piece of chicken that is actually both sides of the breast on a chicken. In a stir-fry, a breast is enough for two or three people. Cornish hens, quail, and squab are smaller, tastier, chicken-like birds. The smaller the bird, the more bones to maneuver around. Duck is a fatty, succulent bird that goes well with many types of sauces: lime and coriander, fruity sauces, or soy-based marinades that are then used later in cooking as reduction sauces.

Dried Foods

In Northern China, foods are dried because of the long winter when there is no food grown. Everything from oysters, shrimp, and beef to mushrooms, yams, and watercress are available dried. Dried foods have an intensified flavor even after they are reconstituted in hot water. Dried mushrooms are used in this book, but other dried foods are not. Use other dried foods in small quantities to flavor dishes if their fresh counterparts are not available. Dried shrimp (not reconstituted) are terrific drizzled atop stir-fried dishes.

Dried Lily Buds

A delicate, musky flavored two-inch-long bud. Soak before using in stir-fried or simmered dishes.

Egg Roll Skins

An egg-and-flour sheet used as a wrapping for egg rolls. Available fresh or frozen in eight-inch squares. Egg rolls are served fried.

Fish

Buying good fresh fish is a skill. The fish should have clear eyes, a clean smell, be firm, and not slimy. Fish to be cooked whole include sea bass, snapper, baby salmon, trout, and black fish. These fish are well-suited to wok cooking.

Meaty fish available in steaks or fillets, such as swordfish, tuna, shark, and salmon, are also well-suited to the fragrant sauces of wok cooking.

Fillets of such fish as sole, cod, and catfish are not often used in this type of cooking, but can be used in recipes that call for small, whole fish.

Meat

The rule is that the shorter the cooking process, the more tender the meat must be. Meat can be tenderized with marinades. In Chinese cooking, all meat is cut against the grain. To slice meat thinly, place wrapped meat in the freezer for fifteen to twenty minutes so that you have a firm slab to cut from (a bit of freezing also works for grating soft cheeses). Chinese cooking uses mostly beef and pork. Fish and chicken are used less often. Buy tender, lean cuts for stir-fried dishes.

Mushrooms

Mushrooms are available fresh, dried, or canned. The most common is the white mushroom, which should be purchased fresh. Dried mushrooms are more flavorful than fresh or canned mushrooms and are well worth finding for your kitchen, especially because they don't easily go bad. Canned mushrooms should be rinsed well before using. Meaty shiitake mushrooms can be purchased fresh or dried. The black mushroom is purchased dry. It retains its caplike shape when dried and is very popular in Chinese cooking. Wood ear or cloud ear mushrooms are dried mushrooms that are strangely clump-shaped. They are not of equal sizes and it is difficult to measure such mushrooms when a recipe calls for a particular number of mushrooms. These mushrooms expand to four to six times their dried size when soaked. Straw mushrooms look like a closed umbrella and are available canned. The fine, delicate, and mild enoki mushrooms are long, thin, white mushrooms with a very small cap. They are sold canned.

Noodles or Pasta

See the chapter on "Noodles and Rice," page 161.

Nuts

Almonds, walnuts, cashews, and peanuts are sautéed, fried, or used as is in recipes. They add a toasted flavor and crunch to recipes. To peel the skin off (blanch) almonds or walnuts, pour boiling water over the nuts. Let sit for two to three minutes for almonds, ten to fifteen minutes for walnuts, then drain and dry, rubbing off the skin. Nuts should be cooked first for a dish because the oil in nuts will be released when cooked and it will flavor the rest of the dish.

Rice

See the chapter on "Noodles and Rice," page 161.

Scallions or Green Onions

Used to garnish many Chinese dishes. Slice in eighth-inch slices for minced scallions.

Shellfish

Squid, a variety of clams, oysters and mussels, crab, shrimp, lobster—these delicacies are the pride of Chinese cooking. They take to sauces well, cook quickly, and offer good flavor.

Shrimp are described in recipes as ''peeled and deveined,'' deveined refers to removing the dark strip of tube running down the back of a shrimp. If not already deveined, cut the back of the shrimp to remove the vein.

Mussels are inexpensive and easy to cook and to eat. Mussels have what is called a beard, a grassy thread that must be pulled off before cooking.

Some varieties of clams include steamers, which are soft-shelled and have a covering on the neck of the clam that is removed after cooking; cherrystone and littleneck clams, which have hard thick shells; razor clams, which are long and slender, with thin, sharp shells, and are terrific for Chinese recipes if you can find them; and geoduck, the largest clam, which is native to the Northwestern United States.

Snow Pea Pods

A flat, edible pea pod. Before cooking, cut off the ends and pull the string from the side of the pod.

Spring Roll Skins

These are similar to egg roll skins, but they contain no egg. Rice-paper wrappers are also called spring roll skins. Spring rolls are lighter in flavor than egg rolls and take less dense fillings and thinner sauces.

Water Chestnuts

This vegetable is added to dishes for its crunchy texture. Purchase canned, whole, or sliced. The water chestnut has only a mild flavor, and it does not absorb the flavor of sauces it is cooked with.

Wonton Skins

These are three-and-a-half-inch-square egg-and-flour sheets for wrapping wontons and dumplings. Good-quality skins can be purchased fresh or frozen. Defrost frozen ones before using. See the Egg Roll or Wonton Skin recipe on page 40.

Seasoning a Wok

Begin by cleaning your new wok thoroughly with soap and water to remove any residual oils that may be in the wok. Some manufacturers recommend rinsing a wok with hot water and letting it soak for an hour, then cleaning it with soap.

Carbon steel and cast-iron woks must be seasoned. These woks will pick up the flavors of the food cooked in them. Nonstick and anodized aluminum woks are not designed to retain flavors from foods cooked in them so they do not have to be seasoned. Many people choose to season them anyway (and the manufacturers of nonstick electric woks do include instructions on seasoning), but there is no evidence that it affects the surface of these woks.

Seasoning a wok is the process of cooking oil into the surface of the wok. It will help to prevent sticking. It will also begin a habit of cooking your wok dry after each use. Water is the enemy of your wok because steel and iron woks can rust. If rust ever appears on your wok, scrub the rust off and reseason the wok.

Place your wok on the stove over medium heat. Add two tablespoons oil. Swirl the oil around the wok. Rub the oil up the sides of the wok using a rag or paper towels. Continue this for about three minutes. Add one more tablespoon oil and rub that into the wok. Cook oil into the wok for two minutes more. Turn off the heat and allow wok to cool. Wipe excess oil off the wok. Now your wok is ready to use.

From now on, you will not need to scour or soap your wok. A wok should be wiped clean and cooked dry after each use. To cook a wok dry, after wiping it clean, put it on a high heat for just a few moments till any moisture on its surface evaporates. Do not use steel wool on any wok. If you need to scrub your wok, a bamboo brush or a plastic scrubber may be used. Over time, your wok might get food burnt onto it. Burnt food will cook off a wok (the same principle is used in self-cleaning ovens), but your wok will not stay clean and pristine. A blackened wok is not an embarrassment but a badge of honor that proclaims you as a well-seasoned wok chef.

Techniques

Blanching

I use blanching for vegetables that are dense and require a longer cooking time than is good for stir-frying. Starchy vegetables, such as potatoes, can release some of their starch through blanching so they don't stick when fried for dishes like hash browns. To blanch, add vegetables to boiling water, then turn the stove off. Stir to evenly heat all the vegetables and let sit for the time prescribed, usually one to five minutes. Drain and pour cold water over the vegetables to stop the cooking. Meats and poultry can also be blanched.

Marinating

Marinating permeates foods with flavor and tenderizes them.

Soup

Serve soup to start the meal.

Heat up six ounces of broth per person, then add one or more of the following for each serving of consomme:

A splash of wine or sherry
A pinch of chopped fresh or dried herbs
A tablespoon of cooked rice or corn
A sliced straw mushroom
A teaspoon or two of chopped tomato, zucchini, or scallion
A tablespoon or two of diced tofu and seaweed

Rice Cooking

Start cooking rice first. Rice is dense, so it will stay warm after it is finished cooking. Give cooked rice a stir, then cover, and set it aside.

Thickening Sauces

Sauces of simmered or stir-fried foods are thickened. Cornstarch should be combined with *cold* liquid for thickening sauces.

Cutting and Chopping

Chinese cutting techniques are meant to expose more of the surface of the food to sauces and heat. Meats are cut against the grain and vegetables are sliced into thin slices for this reason.

Julienne

Cut in wooden matchstick-size pieces, one to two inches long and one-eighth inch in width and depth (large julienne is one-quarter inch).

Cubed or Diced

Usually in half-inch (small) or one-inch (large) cubes.

Shredded Cabbage

Quarter the head of cabbage. Rest the cabbage on one cut side. Cut slices as thinly as possible.

Roll Cut

An attractive cubing technique for cylindrical vegetables such as carrots. Slice at a forty-five-degree angle, roll the carrot a half turn, and cut again at an angle.

Minced

Use mostly for herbs and seasonings such as ginger and garlic. Chop very small. Hold the top of the tip of the knife and chop in an arc back and forth over the food.

Meat

To cut meat into thin slices, freeze for twenty to thirty minutes to firm the meat for easier slicing.

Round Vegetables

To slice round vegetables, cut one slice and then place the cut side down on the cutting surface so that the round vegetable has a flat surface to lean on. Slice as usual. Good for mushrooms and water chestnuts.

Peeling Tomatoes, Peaches, and Almonds

Blanch in boiling water for forty-five seconds. Remove, and rinse in cold water to prevent further cooking. Peel will come off easily.

Broccoli

Don't waste the stem. Peel off the toughest portions of the skin and slice the stem.

Scallions

Scallions are most often sliced in rings cut perpendicular to the length of the scallion. Minced scallions are one-eighth-inch slices. Use only the green part of the scallion for a lighter texture when serving scallions raw (as a garnish). For scallion plumes, slice the end of the scallion along its length, but don't slice off any piece. It will look like fringe. Soak the scallion in cold water. The water will cause the fringed ends to curl.

Garlic

Garlic will peel more easily after the clove is crushed under the flat blade of a cleaver. One other technique is to place unpeeled garlic cloves in water in a sealed container in the refrigerator. The peel will easily rub off, and the garlic will keep this way for weeks.

Garnishes

For color and flavor, try minced parsley or cilantro, minced scallions, or paprika.

Soft small vegetable and fruit fans: Slice, but leave attached at one end. Fan slices at the cut end. Use for strawberries or mushrooms.

Scallion brushes are described above.

For texture, try crumbled nuts, julienned cucumbers, radish, or carrots. Place stir-fry dishes on a bed of deep-fried rice noodles.

PART TWO

RECIPES

Basic Ingredients

The recipes in this chapter are for ingredients that can be purchased already made. Make them from scratch for a fresher flavor, or because you can't find them at your store.

Citrus Peel

Use the peel from any citrus fruit (you might try experimenting with grapefruit or lemons); tangerine is the traditional choice.

Remove any white pith from the underside of the peel. Dry in the sun or in a warm (less than 200°) oven. Store in a covered jar. When you wish to use dried peel, soak it in hot water until it softens.

Five-Spice Powder

There are many variations on the recipe for five-spice powder (a bit more cinnamon, a bit less clove). If you would like to make your own, start with trying:

½ teaspoon whole clove
1 teaspoon whole fennel seed
1 teaspoon whole Szechuan peppercorns
4 star anise *or* 2 teaspoons whole anise seed
2 4-inch segments of cinnamon stick

Pulverize ingredients in a coffee grinder, mortar and pestle, or hammer under a cleaver or rolling pin.

Chili Oil

¼ cup oil
6 whole dried red chilies

Cook oil and chili in a pan over low heat for 20 minutes, then make a small incision in the surface of each chili to help release the flavor. Turn off the stove and allow to cool. Store in a sealed jar for a week before using. If the oil is the right heat for you, discard chilies and continue to use oil. Leave chilies in if you like it even hotter. Add more oil if it is too hot.

Oyster Sauce

1 dozen oysters and their liquid
¼ teaspoon sugar
¼ teaspoon salt
1 teaspoon cornstarch
2 tablespoons soy sauce

Heat oysters, sugar, and salt in a pan. Simmer covered for 15 minutes, stirring occasionally. If there is not enough liquid to cover the oysters, add water. Strain contents well, and discard solids. Return liquid to pan. Combine cornstarch with 1 tablespoon water and mix to remove lumps. Add cornstarch paste and soy sauce to oyster liquid. Stir to blend. Store in a jar in the refrigerator.

Plum Sauce

1 cup plum preserves or jam
¼ cup water
2 tablespoons vinegar
1 garlic clove, peeled and cut in half
2 quarter-size slices of ginger
½ teaspoon salt
½ teaspoon red pepper flakes

Combine ingredients in a pan. Heat to dissolve preserves. Cover and simmer over a low heat, stirring occasionally, for 15 minutes. Remove garlic and ginger. Taste sauce and add sugar if the preserves are not sweet enough. Store in a jar in the refrigerator.

Meat or Poultry Stock

Yield: 1 quart

1–2 pounds beef, lamb, duck, *or* chicken bones
2 cups of any leftover vegetable peels (do not use asparagus, eggplant, or the peels from bitter vegetables such as Chinese broccoli)*
Water
1 bay leaf
3 whole peppercorns
¼ teaspoon salt (if you are making a gallon of stock, just use ½ teaspoon)

Place all bones and vegetables in a roasting pan and roast in a 350° oven for a half hour. Remove and put bones and vegetables in a stockpot and cover with 1 quart plus 1 cup of water. Ingredients should be completely covered with water. Add more water if ingredients are not immersed in water. Add bay leaf and spices and bring to a boil. Cover and reduce heat to low. Simmer 6–8 hours. Skim fat periodically and add more water if liquid evaporates. Strain stock.

*Carrot, onion, celery, turnip, and potato are all terrific for stock. Spinach, parsley, broccoli, cabbage, cauliflower, string beans, mushrooms, cucumber, and tomato are also good for stock.

Fish Stock

Yield: 1 quart

1 pound of shrimp peels, crab and lobster shells, *or* fish bones and skin
1 cup vegetable peels (see meat stock recipe, lighter-colored and -flavored vegetables are best)
1 bay leaf
2 whole peppercorns
¼ teaspoon salt
Water

Place all ingredients in a pot and cover with 1 quart plus 1 cup of water. Bring to a boil, then cover, reduce heat to low, and simmer 1 hour. Strain stock.

Vegetable Stock

Prepare as you would fish stock. Use 3 cups of vegetables. Use 2 cups of garlic, onion, carrot, celery, potato; and use carrot, turnip, and other vegetables for the third cup.

Teriyaki

⅓ cup soy sauce
3 tablespoons brown sugar
2 teaspoons dry mustard
2 teaspoons minced garlic
2 teaspoons minced ginger
2 tablespoons water

Combine ingredients in wok. Heat to dissolve sugar and blend flavors. Pour into a covered jar, and allow to cool. Shake in a covered jar and store in the refrigerator.

Egg Roll or Wonton Skin

2 cups flour
½ teaspoon salt
1 egg, lightly beaten
¼ cup cold water

Combine flour and salt. Add the egg and mix to blend. Add water and blend. Knead lightly, then refrigerate for at least 30 minutes.

Roll out on a floured board as thinly as possible. Cut 3-inch squares for wontons, or 7-inch squares for egg rolls out of the thinly rolled-out area. Coat each skin lightly with cornstarch or flour and stack them until ready to use.

Classics

Everything from popcorn, to omelets, to beef stew are easily made in a wok. Paella and German pancakes are usually made in special pans that are similar in shape to a wok, so why buy a paella pan when you can use your wok? Soups that require a lot of sautéing can be made more easily in a wok. Traditionally, you would sauté in a skillet then finish the soup in a stockpot. With a wok there is only one pot to clean.

Popcorn

Yield: 4–5 cups

¼ cup oil
⅓–½ cup popcorn
Salt, to taste

Heat the wok, add oil, then popcorn. Cover the pan. Cook over a medium heat. Shake the pan to coat the popcorn in oil. When the popcorn begins to pop, shake the wok frequently. When the popping slows and there are 2–3 seconds between pops, remove from the heat. Sprinkle with salt to taste.

Omelets

Serves 2

4 eggs
¼ cup milk
Salt to taste
Pepper to taste
Dash of Tabasco sauce, optional
1 tablespoon butter *or* bacon fat

Omelet Filling (choose two of the following):
¼ cup grated Swiss *or* Cheddar cheese
2 tablespoons chopped tomato
3 slices cooked, crumbled bacon
¼ cup sautéed mushrooms *or* onions
1 slice smoked salmon

Beat eggs lightly. Add milk, salt, pepper, and Tabasco. Beat mixture together.

Heat wok. Add butter to wok over medium heat. When the butter is melted and swirled to coat the wok, add egg mixture. Let the eggs cook until the egg begins to set. Now tip the wok and swirl egg. Lift the edge of the omelet to swirl raw egg under the edge of the omelet. Tip pan long enough to allow omelet to spread over a greater surface of the wok. When all but the very surface of the egg is set, add filling. Fold omelet in half. Cover wok and cook about 1 minute to heat and melt filling. Cut in half and serve.

Ratatouille

Serves 4 as a main dish

3 tablespoons oil
2 teaspoons minced garlic
¼ teaspoon salt
⅔ cup minced onion
1 green pepper, cut in ½-inch dice
1½ pounds eggplant, diced
1 medium zucchini
2 tablespoons red wine
2 large tomatoes, peeled, seeded, and diced
1 tablespoon tomato paste
½ cup tomato juice
1 teaspoon basil
¼ teaspoon thyme
¼ teaspoon rosemary
¼ teaspoon black pepper

Heat wok. When the wok is hot, add oil. When the oil is hot, add the garlic and salt. Give the garlic a quick stir, then reduce the heat to medium. Add onion and pepper and sauté and stir until soft, about 8 minutes. Add eggplant, zucchini, and the wine. Sauté and stir 15 minutes until soft. Stir in tomato, tomato paste, tomato juice, and herbs; cook 5 minutes.

Substitution:
Replace all the tomato products with 1½ cups canned tomatoes and their juice.

Variations:
Thin out the ratatouille with tomato puree and serve on pasta.

Cook off some of the liquid and serve on French rolls.

Use ratatouille to fill an omelet.

Serve as a side dish with lamb.

Spanish Potato Omelet Cake (Tortilla)

Serves 2 for breakfast, 3–4 as appetizer

1 pound baking or new potatoes, peeled and cut
½ cup olive oil
1 clove of garlic, cut in half
5 eggs
¼ teaspoon salt
¼ teaspoon cumin
2 teaspoons minced parsley
⅓ cup minced onion

Peel potatoes and cut in ¼-inch slices.

Heat wok. Add oil to wok. When the oil is hot, add garlic and toss for 30 seconds. Remove garlic when it has flavored the oil. Add potatoes to oil and fry until golden brown. Remove potatoes from wok, drain on paper towels.

Beat the eggs, add salt, cumin, and parsley to the eggs, then place the potatoes in the egg mixture.

While the eggs and potatoes sit, heat the oil left in the wok. Add the onion and fry until soft, but not brown. Remove the onion from the wok, trying to take as little oil with the onion as possible. Add the onion to the eggs and potatoes.

Drain excess oil from the wok, leaving only the lightest coating. Heat wok. Pour egg-potato-onion mixture into the wok and cook covered over a medium heat until set. At the beginning of cooking, shake pan and lift edges of the omelet to prevent sticking.

When most of the omelet is cooked, slide the omelet onto a plate, cover the plate with another plate, and flip. Put the omelet back into the wok to finish on the other side. In about 1 minute it is ready to serve.

Cut in wedges as you would pie, and serve hot or at room temperature.

Lamb Stew

Serves 4

Never make "just enough" stew. It tastes even better the next day, so either make it a day ahead (I refuse to believe that anyone is that organized) or have enough left to eat it tomorrow, too.

This recipe evolved from a Swedish leg of lamb recipe that had a terrific gravy. I turned it into a stew to put that gravy center stage.

5–6 new potatoes, peeled and quartered
2 carrots, peeled and cut in 1-inch segments
2 pounds cubed lamb for stew
3 tablespoons butter
1 medium onion, cut in ½-inch dice
2 tablespoons flour
1 teaspoon rosemary, crushed
½ teaspoon salt
¾ cup red wine
1 cup coffee
½ cup cream
½ tablespoon sugar
¾ cup chicken broth

Blanch potatoes and carrots in boiling water for 5 minutes.

Brown lamb in 2 tablespoons butter. Remove lamb from wok. Add 1 tablespoon butter to wok and sauté onion 1 minute. Add flour and cook 2 minutes more. Add rosemary, salt, and wine. Stir to blend wine with flour, cook 2–3 minutes until liquid is slightly thickened.

Add the rest of the ingredients to the wok. Stir to blend. Bring to just under a boil, then add lamb, cover, and simmer for 1 hour.

Onion Soup

Serves 4

4 tablespoons butter
4 cups thinly sliced onions
¼ cup white wine
1 teaspoon dried thyme
½ teaspoon dried mustard
Salt, to taste
Pepper, to taste
1 quart vegetable stock or water

Accompaniments:
Toasted croutons
Grated Parmesan
Grated or sliced Swiss cheese (melt grated cheese by stirring it into each serving of soup or toast slices of cheese on each serving of soup in the oven)

Melt butter in wok. Sauté onions over medium heat until very soft and translucent. Do not brown. Add wine to deglaze wok. Add thyme, mustard, salt, and pepper, then add stock. Stir well and simmer covered for 30 minutes.

Serve with toasted bread croutons and grated cheese.

Macaroni and Cheese

Serves 4

Try the variations. I never add the same things twice, but I always add something.

1 pound macaroni, prepared according to package directions
5 tablespoons butter
2 tablespoons flour
2 cups warmed milk
1 cup grated cheese, your preference (try a combination of sharp Cheddar and Parmesan)
Salt to Taste
Pepper to taste
1 dash cayenne pepper
1 dash nutmeg

Prepare macaroni according to package directions. While macaroni is cooking, melt 3 tablespoons of the butter in the wok. Add flour and stir constantly for 2 minutes. Add the milk, and beat with a whisk until smooth. Cook over a low heat for 10 minutes until slightly thickened. Keep stirring. Add cheese and seasonings. Stir to melt cheese. When the cheese is melted, add 2 tablespoons butter and stir to melt butter. Toss with pasta and serve.

Variations:
Add up to a cup of onions, mushrooms, or peppers (or a combination) to the melted butter before adding the flour and sauté until soft, then add the flour.

Add ½ cup chopped scallions and/or fresh tomato to the sauce when you add the cheese.

Add 1 tablespoon chopped, poached, or sun-dried tomato *or* 2 tablespoons chopped chives to the sauce, when adding the macaroni.

Dutch Oven Pancake

Serves 2 for breakfast

This dish is usually cooked in a pancake pan that looks just like a wok, so I have always used my wok. You cannot have any plastic or rubber handles on your wok, because the wok is put in the oven for this recipe.

Notice how the proportions in the recipe are 1 egg, to ¼ cup milk, to ¼ cup flour, etc. I have made this recipe for one with two eggs in a small bowl, or for 4 for breakfast with 6 eggs in a wok.

A German oven pancake is custardy like a popover on the inside and crisp on the outside.

3 eggs
¾ cup milk
¾ cup flour
¼ teaspoon salt
1 tablespoon butter

Preheat the oven to 450°.

Combine the eggs, milk, flour, and salt. Stir until smooth.

Heat the wok. Melt the butter in the wok. Swirl to coat pan. Pour in the batter. Bake for 15 minutes. Reduce heat to 350° and bake 10 minutes more to set the inside of the pancake.

Traditionally served with apples sautéed in butter and seasoned with cinnamon and sugar. It is also good with warmed applesauce or maple syrup. For a **Quick Fruit Compote,** use canned fruit, a pinch of spices and some sweet wine (for example, 1 16-ounce can of peaches, rinsed; ¼ teaspoon nutmeg; ¼ cup port—simmer 10 minutes).

Picadillo Stuffed Cabbage

Serves 4

Picadillo is a Caribbean ground beef dish intensely flavored with capers, olives, and raisins for elements of salt and sweet. It has always reminded me of the filling my great aunt uses in her stuffed cabbage. I added a bit of cooked rice to the picadillo and topped the stuffed cabbage with a light tomato sauce flavored with vinegar and sugar.

¼ cup raisins
¼ cup dark rum
2 cups water
1 head of cabbage (This recipe uses only the outer leaves. After the cabbage is parboiled, save the rest for another use.)
2 tablespoons olive oil
1 teaspoon minced garlic
½ teaspoon red pepper flakes
½ onion, minced
½ green pepper, seeded and finely chopped
½ pound ground beef
½ pound ground pork
1 28-ounce can of whole plum tomatoes
¼ teaspoon ground cumin
⅛ teaspoon cinnamon
½ teaspoon salt
¼ teaspoon ground pepper
¼ cup pimiento-stuffed olives, minced
1 tablespoon capers
1 cup cooked rice
1 cup beef stock
1 teaspoon brown sugar
2 teaspoons vinegar

Soak the raisins in the rum. Set aside.

Bring 2 cups of water to a boil in the wok. Place the whole cabbage, stem side down, in the water. Cover and boil 5 minutes. Remove the cabbage from the wok and set aside.

Heat wok. When the wok is hot, add oil. Reduce the heat to medium, and add garlic and red pepper flakes. Stir to flavor the oil. Add onion and green pepper and stir to coat with oil. Add ground meat and brown, about 4 minutes. Remove from the wok to a large bowl. Strain off any excess oil. Mince 4 of the tomatoes. Add the chopped tomato, cumin, cinnamon, and ¼ teaspoon salt and the pepper. Add the raisins (save the rum), pimiento-stuffed olives, and capers. Stir in the rice.

Remove cabbage leaves carefully from the head. Cut the leaf away at the stem. Cut off any thickened ribs on the leaf, being careful not to pierce the leaf.

Place a leaf on your work surface. Place about ¼ cup of the meat and rice filling about two inches in from the stem end. Fold the stem end over the filling. Fold each of the sides in over the filling, then fold or roll the tip over the cabbage and place the bundle in the wok. Repeat until all the filling and whole cabbage leaves are used (makes about 12 cabbage bundles). Save the rest of the cabbage for another use.

Chop the rest of the tomatoes. Combine tomatoes and their juice with the rum from the raisins, the beef broth, brown sugar, vinegar, and ¼ teaspoon salt, and pour over the cabbage bundles. Cover and simmer 45 minutes.

Variations:

If you prefer a firmer cabbage bundle, add 1 raw egg to the filling.

Paella

Serves 6

Since a paella pan looks like a slightly flattened wok, a wok is a perfect substitute. When the paella is done, bring the wok to the table. It makes for a wonderful and impressive presentation.

¼ cup oil
3 garlic cloves, cut in half
1 chicken, cut in 8 pieces
1 pound Spanish sausage (chorizo *or* linguica)—if unavailable, use Italian pork sausage, cut on the diagonal in 1-inch-thick slices
1½ cups short-grain rice
¼ cup red wine
3½ cups chicken stock
1 teaspoon saffron, crushed
2 bay leaves
1 teaspoon thyme
1 teaspoon rosemary
2 teaspoons pepper
2 teaspoons salt
1 28-ounce can of tomatoes
2 cups coarsely chopped onion
2 sweet red peppers, cut in 1-inch dice
1 pound shrimp, peeled and deveined, leave the tail on
12 littleneck clams, scrubbed clean
1½ cups peas
¼ cup chopped parsley
3 lemons, quartered
3 limes, quartered

Heat the wok. Add oil. When the oil is hot, add the garlic, then the chicken. Brown the chicken in the oil, about 15 minutes. If the garlic begins to brown, remove it from the oil and discard. Remove the chicken from the wok. Set aside. Discard the garlic. Brown sausage in the wok, then set aside.

Add the rice to the wok and sauté 2 minutes. Add red wine, ½ cup of the chicken stock, the saffron, and the bay leaves to the wok. Stir into the rice. Add the rest of the spices, the tomatoes, and the rest of the chicken stock. Bring to a boil.

Add the chicken, sausage, onion, and peppers. Cover and simmer 30 minutes, stirring once after about 10 minutes. Place the shrimp and clams on top. Drizzle with peas. Cover and simmer 5 minutes. Garnish with parsley, lemon, and lime. Instruct your guests to squeeze the citrus on the paella.

Variations:

Use rabbit instead of chicken.

Use mussels instead of clams.

Use firm fish such as halibut or swordfish instead of shrimp.

Replace some of the sausage with a salty ham such as Tasso.

Use lima beans instead of peas.

Replace some of the chicken stock with bottled clam broth.

Beef Stew with Red Wine

Serves 6

3 tablespoons butter or bacon fat
2 pounds beef cut in 1-inch cubes
2 shallots
8 ounces halved mushrooms
3 tablespoons flour
2 cups dry red wine
1 teaspoon salt
⅛ teaspoon pepper
½ teaspoon thyme
1 bay leaf
4 medium carrots, cut in ¾-inch pieces
6 red potatoes, quartered
12 pearl onions, peeled
2 cups beef stock

Heat the wok. Add butter. When butter is hot, add the beef and brown on all sides. Remove beef from the wok and set aside. Add the shallots and mushrooms to wok. Sauté over medium-low heat for 5 minutes. Add flour, and stir to brown flour.

Add wine and seasonings. Stir to blend and thicken. Add carrots, potatoes, and onions, add beef and beef stock. Bring to a boil. Reduce heat to low, cover, and simmer 1½ hours.

Garlic Shrimp

Serves 4 as an appetizer

Served as an appetizer, it is a Spanish tapa dish; put it on pasta and it is scampi.

4 tablespoons olive oil
4 teaspoons chopped garlic
1 pound shrimp, peeled and deveined
1½ tablespoons lemon juice
2 tablespoons sherry
½ teaspoon cumin
¼ teaspoon paprika
½ teaspoon oregano
⅛ teaspoon red pepper flakes
⅛ teaspoon salt
⅛ teaspoon pepper
4 slices toasted bread, cut in half to form two triangles
1 tablespoon chopped parsley

Heat wok. When the wok is hot, add oil, reduce heat to medium-low, and add garlic. Sauté garlic for 2 minutes. Add shrimp and toss with garlic, then add the rest of the ingredients except the toast and parsley. Cook and toss 3 minutes until shrimp is just cooked through. Arrange on toast points and garnish with parsley.

Stir-Fried Fajitas

Serves 4

Finger food is always a hit in my house. This recipe uses both beef and chicken to please the tastes of different people.

½ cup lime juice
¼ cup soy sauce
½ cup Worcestershire sauce
¼ teaspoon Tabasco sauce
¼ teaspoon cumin
⅛ teaspoon ground coriander
1 boneless chicken breast, cut in ½-inch-wide strips
½ pound beef, cut in ½-inch-wide strips
2 peppers, cut in ½-inch-wide strips
1 onion, cut in ¼-inch-wide strips
4 tablespoons oil
2 cups boiling water
8 flour tortillas

Accompaniments:
Sliced avocado
Thin wedges of tomato
Salsa
Sour cream

Combine lime juice, soy, Worcestershire, Tabasco, cumin, and coriander. Marinate chicken, beef, peppers, and onion for at least 1 hour, separately.

Heat wok. When the wok is hot, add 2 tablespoons oil. When the oil is hot, add the peppers and onions. Stir-fry about 4 minutes until tender. Remove from the wok. Now cook the beef about 2 minutes, and after that the chicken about 2 minutes, until opaque and cooked through. Remove and keep the vegetables, beef, and chicken warm.

Wipe out wok, and add 2 cups boiling water. Loosely roll tortillas and steam 1–2 minutes. Steam meat and vegetables for 1 minute if they have gotten cold.

Arrange cooked food on one plate with the tortillas. Arrange accompaniments on another plate. To make a fajita, take a tortilla and fill with meat, vegetables, and accompaniments along the center. Fold the bottom of the tortilla up and roll in the sides over the filling. Try to eat without making a mess.

Stove-Top Tamale Pie

Serves 4

¼ teaspoon salt
½ pound beef
1 onion, chopped in ½-inch dice
1 pepper, cut in ½-inch dice
½ cup canned posole, rinsed
½ cup beans (kidney beans or your favorite)
½ teaspoon oregano
1 teaspoon cumin
½ teaspoon coriander
⅛ teaspoon cayenne
1½ cups chopped, canned tomato
½ cup sour cream
½ cup prepared salsa
¾ cup cornmeal

Heat wok, and add salt. Add beef, and brown for 1 minute. Add onion and pepper and stir-fry until beef is browned and onion is translucent and soft. Drain fat from wok. Add the posole and beans, then the spices. Spoon the tomato, sour cream, and salsa over top, and then sprinkle the cornmeal on. Cover with foil and then the wok lid and simmer on low for 20 minutes. Check after 10 minutes. If the cornmeal is still dry, sprinkle with ¼ cup water. Cover and continue cooking.

Variations:
Cover the top of the pie with cheese instead of foil.

Posole is whole hominy. If you can't find it, replace it with corn.

Add chopped jalapeño if you like your food spicy.

Use ground turkey instead of beef.

Leftover meat from Barbecue Pork Sandwiches (page 155) can be substituted for the beef in this recipe.

Wok-Fried Snack Mix

Yield: 4 cups

¼ cup butter
1 teaspoon cumin
½ teaspoon paprika
2 teaspoons Worcestershire sauce
¼ teaspoon Tabasco sauce
2 teaspoons soy sauce
2 cups nuts, your choice (try a combination of peanuts, almonds, and pecans)
2 cups small pretzels

Melt butter in wok. Add cumin, paprika, Worcestershire, Tabasco, and soy sauce. Stir to blend flavors. Add nuts, and sauté over medium heat for 2–3 minutes until they are lightly toasted. Add pretzels and toss. Nuts soften when heated, so allow to cool thoroughly before serving. Store in an airtight container.

Variation:
Add 2 cups of your favorite unsweetened cereal.

Asparagus

Asparagus spears are wonderful steamed, but before I bought a steamer, I found an even better way to cook asparagus in my wok. All the asparagus are placed in the wok with the tips pointing up the side of the wok and the tougher end of the stalk at the center of the wok. The asparagus is placed in the wok after 2 cups of water come to a boil in the wok. The wok is covered, then the stove is turned off. Allow to sit covered for 12–15 minutes, depending on the thickness of the asparagus.

Stir-Frying

Stir-frying was developed by the Cantonese. Their dishes were mildly seasoned and slightly undercooked to preserve the flavor and color of the food. Sauces for the stir-fry were created by thickening broth with cornstarch.

More recently, other types of stir-fries have developed using the spicy chilies of Szechuan and the dried mushrooms of Peking.

The principle of stir-frying is to cook food quickly over a high heat. Stir-fry recipes are never made in large quantities because it would slow down the cooking process and ruin the stir-fry. All ingredients for a stir-fry must be set out and ready before you begin to cook. The cooking itself will happen too quickly for there to be time to look for a forgotten ingredient without overcooking the food. In many of the recipes it will say, "add" this, "then add" that. The time interval between when you add the first ingredient and when you add the second is a few moments, 10 seconds at the most. Garlic and ginger are added to the oil at the very beginning to flavor the oil, but must only be stirred for a few moments before adding the next ingredient. Cooking it longer will burn the garlic and make it taste bitter. The seasoning for a stir-fry is often divided; half of the seasonings are used to marinate the meat or fish, and half are mixed with liquid and cornstarch to be added at the end to form the sauce for the dish.

To stir-fry, you must begin by heating your wok. Heat the wok over a high heat for 30 seconds, then add a small amount of oil, and you are ready to cook. Peanut oil doesn't smoke or burn as easily as other oils, but any light-flavored cooking oil will suffice. A stir-fry must be stirred constantly. Stir with one hand and add ingredients with the other hand. Liquid is added at the end of cooking. The food is pushed away from the center of the wok and the liquid is poured into that hole. The heat is reduced slightly as the sauce thickens and glazes the food. There is heat in the wok and the food even after the stove is turned off. The heat in the food will continue to cook it, even after it is removed from the wok, so stir-fried dishes must be served immediately.

No food item needs more than five minutes in the wok. Foods are cut small so they cook quickly. Hard vegetables such as carrots, broccoli, cauliflower, cabbage, and asparagus should be blanched before stir-frying to reduce the time they need to cook in the wok. Even meats can be blanched if you wish to use a thicker cut.

Some of the ingredients you'll need to season your stir-fries are garlic and fresh ginger, soy sauce, dry sherry wine, white wine, rice wine, Oyster Sauce (page 37) and, of course, salt and pepper. Some other special ingredients such as intensely flavored salted black beans, dried mushrooms, hot Chili Oil (page 36), and the complexly flavored Five-Spice Powder (page 36) are also used in stir-fries. This chapter includes recipes on how to use each of these ingredients in a stir-fry.

When I wrote this cookbook, I learned a few things that I might not have found out any other way. I developed a system for making stir-fries that you might find helpful. I stir-fry in two shifts. I clean, cut, and season all my ingredients as soon as I arrive home. I put the rice on to cook and then I take time out to watch TV or read the newspaper. Later, when it is time for dinner, I serve a soup or cold dish, depending on the weather, and then I make the stir-fry. It only takes a few minutes so no one minds, especially because they have already eaten a bit of food. It is a very civilized cooking schedule that keeps me from feeling like I am always in the kitchen.

Chicken with Orange Sauce and Broccoli

Serves 3

This was one of my first stir-fry dishes. It was only when my family tired of it that I started to create the other recipes in this book.

1 boneless chicken breast, cut in 1-inch-wide strips
2 teaspoons soy sauce
1 teaspoon lemon juice

Sauce:
4 tablespoons orange juice
2 teaspoons gin
2 teaspoons soy sauce (1 tablespoon in total needed for recipe)
1 teaspoon sesame oil
Dash of Tabasco sauce
1 teaspoon cornstarch

2 tablespoons oil
1 teaspoon garlic
¾ cup julienned cabbage (sliced thinly)
1½ cups broccoli

Combine chicken, 2 teaspoons of soy sauce, and lemon juice in a small bowl. Set aside.

Combine sauce ingredients in a small bowl. Stir until cornstarch is dissolved. Set aside.

Heat wok, then add oil and garlic. Give garlic a quick stir and then add cabbage and broccoli florets and 1-inch pieces of peeled broccoli. Cook 2 minutes over medium-high heat. Add chicken and toss to cook. Cook 3 minutes, then add sauce. Cook 1–2 minutes until sauce thickens and chicken is cooked through.

Five-Spiced Pork with Cabbage and Peppers

Serves 3

Marinade:

1 tablespoon soy sauce
½ tablespoon cornstarch
½ teaspoon Five-Spice Powder (see recipe on page 36)
¼ teaspoon salt
1 tablespoon sherry

½ pound lean pork, sliced thinly and against the grain
2 tablespoons oil
1 cup shredded cabbage
1 sweet red pepper, sliced in ¼-inch-wide strips
½ cup snow peas
⅓ cup beef stock
1 tablespoon soy sauce

Combine marinade ingredients. Add pork to marinade and toss to coat. Let marinate for 30 minutes, tossing occasionally.

Heat oil in wok. Add pork, and cook until just browned. Remove pork from wok.

Add cabbage and peppers to wok and stir-fry for 2 minutes. Add snow peas and pork. Stir in stock and soy sauce. Simmer for 2 minutes more over medium heat.

Stir-Fried Spareribs

Serves 4

1 teaspoon cornstarch
2 teaspoons soy sauce
2 tablespoons *plus* ⅓ cup water
¼ cup sugar
¼ cup vinegar
2 teaspoons tomato paste
¼ cup oil
2 pounds pork spareribs, cut in 1 inch bite-size pieces, cut right through the bone (ask the butcher to do it)

Combine cornstarch, soy sauce, and 2 tablespoons water. Set aside.

Bring ⅓ cup water to a boil in the wok. Add sugar, stir until dissolved, then add vinegar and tomato paste. Add cornstarch paste. Mixture will thicken just slightly. Remove from wok and set aside.

Heat wok. When the wok is hot, add oil. When oil is hot, add ribs until browned, 6–8 minutes. Drain off any oil left in the pan. Add sauce and toss to coat. Any excess sauce can be used for dipping.

Winter Vegetable Stir-Fry

Serves 3 as a main dish or 6 as a side dish

½ cup carrots, sliced thinly on the diagonal
1 cup shredded cabbage
6 dried black mushrooms, soaked in ½ cup water and sliced thinly (reserve water)
1 tablespoon cornstarch
3 teaspoons minced ginger
1 tablespoon soy sauce
½ teaspoon sugar
2 tablespoons oil
1 teaspoon minced garlic
1 cup broccoli florets

Blanch carrots and cabbage in water for 4 minutes.

Combine mushroom water, cornstarch, ginger, soy sauce, and sugar. Set aside.

Heat wok. When hot, add oil. When the oil is hot, add the garlic, then the broccoli and mushrooms. Cook 2 minutes, then add carrots and cabbage and cook 2 minutes more. Make room at the center of the wok and add sauce. Bring liquid to a boil. Cook until sauce thickens.

Gingered Beef with Asparagus

Serves 4

1 teaspoon fresh ginger, minced
2 tablespoons sherry
1 teaspoon soy sauce
1 pound beef, sliced thinly and against the grain
2 tablespoons oil
2 quarter-size slices of ginger
¾ pound asparagus, cut in 2-inch segments, blanched for 1 minute
¼ cup beef stock
1 teaspoon cornstarch

Combine ginger, sherry, and soy sauce. Add beef and toss to coat. Set aside for 15 minutes.

Heat wok, then add oil. When the oil is hot, add ginger and stir-fry for 30 seconds. Add beef and asparagus and stir-fry until beef is just browned, 2 minutes. Mix beef stock and cornstarch until smooth. Add beef stock mixture, bring to a boil. Cook 2 minutes until sauce thickens and beef and asparagus are cooked through. Remove ginger slices.

Cantonese Stir-Fry

Serves 2

A light, simple dish such as this should not be served alone. It is mild and typical of Cantonese food, but in my mind it needs a spicy side dish to complement it.

1 tablespoon rice wine
1 tablespoon light soy sauce
1 teaspoon sugar
1 boneless chicken breast, cubed
1 teaspoon cornstarch
½ cup chicken stock
2 tablespoons oil
3 scallions, minced
1 cup zucchini cubes (slice zucchini in ½-inch slices, then cut each slice into 6 wedges)

Drizzle rice wine, soy sauce, and sugar over chicken and toss to coat.

Combine cornstarch and chicken stock and set aside.

Heat wok. Add 1 tablespoon oil. When oil is hot, add chicken and brown on all sides. Remove chicken from wok.

Return wok to heat and add 1 more tablespoon oil. When the oil is hot, add scallions and zucchini and stir-fry 1 minute, then return chicken to wok. Add chicken stock mixture and bring to a boil. Reduce heat to medium. Cook to coat and thicken, about 2 minutes.

Sweet and Sour Beef with Peppers

Serves 2

Sauce:

2 tablespoons sugar
2 tablespoons vinegar
1 tablespoon soy sauce
1 tablespoon water
½ tablespoon tomato paste
1 teaspoon cornstarch
Dash of Tabasco sauce

½ pound lean beef, cut in 1-inch cubes
1½ tablespoons oil
1 garlic clove, peeled and halved
1⅛ -inch slice of ginger
1 green pepper, seeded and cubed
½ 8-ounce can sliced bamboo shoots, rinsed

Combine sauce ingredients and add beef. Toss and let stand for 15 minutes. Remove beef from marinade and reserve marinade.

Heat wok. When the wok is hot, add oil. When the oil is hot, add garlic and ginger, then beef. Stir-fry until browned, 2–3 minutes. Remove beef. Dispose of garlic and ginger.

Reheat pan and add peppers and bamboo shoots. Stir-fry 1 minute. Add beef marinade. Bring to a boil. Return beef to the wok, reduce heat, and simmer 1 minute. Serve immediately.

Chicken, Corn, and Red Pepper, a Stir-Fry for the August Moon

Serves 3

Only once a year is the corn sweet and ready for the pickin' and the sweet red peppers inexpensive and grown locally. This is one of those recipes that grew out of necessity. I went hog-wild at the farmers' market and came home with too much corn and too many peppers, so I developed this recipe to make use of the bounty.

Sauce:

1 tablespoon cornstarch
¼ cup sherry
2 tablespoons soy sauce
2 tablespoons water
1½ tablespoon minced Chinese parsley (cilantro)
½ teaspoon sugar

2½ tablespoons oil
1 teaspoon minced garlic
1 teaspoon minced ginger
¼ cup minced onion
1 boneless chicken breast, cut in 1-inch-wide strips
2 red peppers, seeded and cut in ½-inch-wide strips
1 cup fresh corn, cut from the cob (about two ears)
1 tablespoon minced scallions

Combine sauce ingredients and set aside.

Heat wok. Add 1½ tablespoons oil. When the oil is hot, add the garlic, ginger, and onion. Cook 30 seconds. Add chicken and stir-fry about 3 minutes. Keep everything moving or the onion and garlic will burn. Remove chicken and onions from the wok.

Add 1 more tablespoon oil, and don't worry about the

bits of onion that are still in the wok. Add red pepper to wok. Stir-fry 1 minute, then add corn. Stir-fry 1 minute more. Add sauce and return chicken to wok. Stir to coat ingredients as sauce thickens and glazes the dish; cook 1 minute. Garnish with scallions. Serve immediately.

Chicken and Walnuts

Serves 4

1 teaspoon sugar
3 tablespoons sherry
1 tablespoon soy sauce
1 teaspoon Worcestershire sauce
2 boneless chicken breasts, cut in 1-inch-wide strips
¼ cup cornstarch
1 lightly beaten egg
2 tablespoons oil
1 cup walnuts
2 teaspoons minced garlic
2 teaspoons minced ginger
½ cup sliced bamboo shoots
½ cup water chestnuts
⅔ cup water

Combine sugar, sherry, soy sauce, and Worcestershire. Add chicken and toss. Let stand 30 minutes.

Drain chicken and save the marinade. Set marinade aside. Dredge chicken in cornstarch, then egg.

Heat oil in wok. Reduce heat to medium and sauté walnuts in oil until just lightly browned. Remember that nuts burn easily. Remove walnuts and drain on paper towels. Add garlic and ginger, then chicken. Stir-fry 3 minutes until chicken is opaque. Add bamboo shoots and water chestnuts, then water and the chicken marinade. Bring to a boil, cover, and reduce heat to medium-low. Simmer 15 minutes, stirring occasionally. Add nuts and serve.

Sweet and Sour Chicken with Autumn Colors

Serves 4

Sauce:

1 16-ounce can of pineapple chunks, drained; reserve ½ cup of the liquid and add to the sauce.
2 tablespoons cornstarch
½ cup vinegar
2 tablespoons roasted red pepper, diced
¼ cups sugar
2 tablespoons orange marmalade

2 tablespoons oil
2 boneless chicken breasts, cut in 1-inch-wide strips
1 green pepper, seeded and cut in 1-inch-wide strips
1 medium onion, sliced in thin rings

Combine sauce ingredients. Set aside.

Heat oil in hot wok. Stir-fry chicken 3 minutes until opaque. Add green pepper and onion, and stir-fry 1–2 minutes more. Stir in sauce. Bring to a boil, then reduce heat to medium-low. Simmer 15 minutes, stirring occasionally.

Beef and Chinese Cabbage with Oyster Sauce

Serves 2

2 teaspoons soy sauce
2 teaspoons sherry
2 tablespoons cornstarch
½ pound beef, sliced thinly against the grain of the meat
¼ cup beef stock (see recipe on page 38)
1 tablespoon Oyster Sauce (see recipe on page 37)
2 tablespoons oil
3 cups Chinese cabbage

Combine soy sauce, sherry, and 1 tablespoon cornstarch. Toss with beef and let stand 15 minutes.

Combine beef stock, 1 tablespoon cornstarch, and oyster sauce. Set aside.

Heat 1 tablespoon oil in wok. Add beef and stir-fry 2 minutes until browned. Remove beef from pan.

Heat second tablespoon of oil in wok. Stir-fry cabbage 1–2 minutes. Add beef stock sauce and beef. Bring to a boil, and cook 1–2 minutes until sauce thickens and glazes beef and cabbage.

Mu Shu Pork

Serves 3

Marinade:

1 tablespoon soy sauce
½ teaspoon sugar
1 tablespoon sherry
¼ teaspoon salt
1 tablespoon cornstarch

½ pound lean pork, sliced thinly against the grain (pieces should be no wider than ½ inch)
3½ tablespoons oil
2 eggs, beaten
1 teaspoon ginger
2 cups cabbage
6 dried black mushrooms, soaked in boiling water, drained, sliced; reserve 1 tablespoon of the mushroom water
¼ cup bamboo shoots
3 scallions, sliced on the diagonal in 1-inch lengths
2 tablespoons Hoisin sauce

Combine marinade ingredients and add pork. Let marinate for 15 minutes.

Heat wok and add ½ tablespoon oil. Swirl oil to coat sides. If after swirling there is any leftover oil, pour it out. Add eggs. Allow eggs to set for a few moments, then swirl to spread egg out. Keep swirling, spreading egg out to form a thin film on the wok. Turn off heat before egg becomes dry, but wait until it is set. The egg will cook a bit after the heat is turned off. Carefully loosen the rim of the sheet of egg. Fold the sheet in quarters and remove from the pan. Let the egg cool, then slice in ½-by-1½-inch pieces.

Heat 1 tablespoon oil in wok, then add ginger. Toss ginger quickly in oil. Add pork and stir-fry 3 minutes. Remove from wok. Scrape out any pieces of gristle that are still in the wok.

Reheat wok and add 2 tablespoons oil. Add cabbage and stir-fry 1 minute. Add mushrooms and bamboo shoots and stir-fry a minute more. Add pork, egg strips, scallions. Hoisin sauce, and mushroom water. Stir and toss to coat with the Hoisin sauce.

Serve with Mu Shu pancakes (below) and plum sauce.

Mu Shu Pancakes

Yield: 12 pancakes

This is the simplest flat recipe there is. It is quite similar to the recipe for Mexican flour tortillas. For a different version, use the egg roll recipe in the Ingredients chapter and panfry.

2 cups flour
¾ cup boiling water

Place flour in a bowl. Add the boiling water gradually. Stir until blended. When cool, knead lightly. Roll the dough into a foot-long cylinder with your hands. Cut off a 1-inch piece. Form dough into a patty about 2 inches in diameter. Lightly oil and flour the patty. Place the patty on a floured surface and roll out to form a circle about 7–8 inches in diameter. Repeat with the rest of the dough. Stack the pancakes with waxed paper between them. Keep them away from the heat.

Tips on rolling:
Roll from the center out.

Give the dough a quarter turn after rolling to insure that it isn't sticking and to roll a more circular pancake.

Flip the dough over when the rolling is half done and continue rolling on the flip side.

Flour as necessary to keep from sticking.

Cook pancakes lightly in a frying pan or on a griddle that is very lightly oiled (oil, and then wipe off the oil). Cook 20–30 seconds per side. They can be cooked in a flat-bottomed wok.

Beef with Tomato

Serves 4

Marinade:

¼ cup beef broth (see page 38)
1 tablespoon soy sauce
1 tablespoon cornstarch
½ teaspoon vinegar
Dash of Tabasco sauce

¾ pound lean beef, sliced thinly against the grain
3 tablespoons oil
1 teaspoon garlic
½ cup onion, cut in slivers
1 green pepper, seeded and cut in 1-inch cubes
2 cups of tomato wedges (2 medium tomatoes)

Combine marinade with beef and let stand at least 15 minutes.

Heat wok, add 2 tablespoons oil, then add garlic to flavor oil. Stir-fry onion and peppers 2 minutes. Remove vegetables from wok.

Strain beef and reserve marinade. Add 1 tablespoon oil to hot wok. Brown beef in wok about 2 minutes. Add tomato and give it a quick stir, then return onion and peppers to wok. Push food to sides of the wok and pour marinade into the center. Bring sauce to a boil. Stir sauce into vegetables and beef and allow sauce to thicken and glaze food.

Chinese Beef and Onion Sandwiches

Serves 3

Marinade:
1 tablespoon soy sauce
1 teaspoon sugar
1 tablespoon sherry
½ tablespoon cornstarch
½ teaspoon dry mustard

¾ pound beef, sliced thinly against the grain
1½ cups sliced onions
1½ tablespoons cornstarch
4 tablespoons oil
1 tablespoon tomato paste
¼ cup beef stock (see page 38)
1 teaspoon vinegar
½ cup sesame oil

Combine marinade ingredients and add beef. Let stand 15 minutes.

Toss onions with cornstarch. Heat wok. Add 3 tablespoons oil, then onions. Stir-fry 3 minutes until onions are soft and translucent. Remove from wok.

Add 1 tablespoon oil to hot wok. Add beef, and brown 2 minutes. Return onions to wok. Combine tomato paste, beef stock, vinegar, and sesame oil. Add sauce to wok. Stir to coat.

Serve on French rolls.

Wok-Fried Squid

Serves 4 as an appetizer

While this is not really a Chinese dish, this recipe incorporates the same principles. This dish is fragrant and colorful, and uses the light, fresh seasonings of Cantonese cooking.

1½ pounds squid, cleaned and sliced in 1-inch rings
¼ cup basil, coarsely chopped
¼ cup parsley, coarsely chopped
2 tablespoons oil
1 tablespoon garlic, chopped
1 small, sweet red pepper, diced
1 scallion, minced
Crushed red pepper
1 bunch watercress, cleaned and arranged on four plates

Combine squid, basil, and parsley.

Heat wok over high flame for 30 seconds. Reduce heat to medium and add oil. Hold wok and swirl to coat pan with the oil. Add garlic, stir, then add squid mixture. Stir again and add pepper and scallion. Add crushed red pepper to taste. Cook 2–3 minutes, until squid is opaque. Season with salt, or lemon juice if you wish to cut down on salt.

Serve on the watercress as a first course.

Scallop Stir-Fry with Oyster Sauce

Serves 4

Sauce:

½ cup chicken *or* fish stock (see page 39) *or* bottled clam broth
2 tablespoons Oyster Sauce (see page 37)
1 tablespoon cornstarch
1 tablespoon white wine

2½ tablespoons oil
1 cup zucchini *or* yellow summer squash, very thinly sliced
½ pound mushrooms, thinly sliced
6 ounces snow peas
1 1-×-½-inch dried orange peel (see page 35), soaked in hot water for a half hour
2 quarter-size slices of fresh ginger
½ pound scallops, sliced in half to form thin discs
4 scallions, minced
½ teaspoon soy sauce
½ teaspoon sesame oil

Combine sauce ingredients, then set aside. Heat wok, add 1½ tablespoons oil. When hot, add zucchini and mushrooms and stir-fry 2–3 minutes. Add snow peas and stir-fry 1 minute more, until peas turn bright green. Remove from wok.

Reheat wok and add 1 tablespoon oil. Add orange peel and ginger to hot oil and stir-fry 30 seconds. Add scallops and scallions. Stir-fry 1–2 minutes until scallops are opaque. Push scallops away from the center of the wok. Pour sauce into the center of the wok and bring to a boil. Return vegetables to wok, add soy sauce and sesame oil, and stir to coat. Remove ginger and orange peel. Terrific served on noodles.

Spicy Tofu and Broccoli with Sesame Sauce

Serves 4

Marinade:

2 tablespoons soy sauce
1 tablespoon cornstarch
2 tablespoons cold water
1 teaspoon chili oil

½ pound firm tofu, cut in ½-inch cubes
¼ cup sesame paste
1 tablespoon vinegar
¼ cup water
A shake or two of chili oil, to taste
2 tablespoons oil
1 bunch of broccoli, cut into florets, the stems peeled and sliced thinly on the diagonal and blanched in boiling water for 1 minute
1 tablespoon cornstarch
2 tablespoons water
2 tablespoons toasted sesame seeds

Combine marinade ingredients. When cornstarch has dissolved in marinade, add tofu. Marinate overnight.

Combine sesame paste, vinegar, ¼ cup water, and chili oil.

Drain tofu carefully and reserve marinade. Heat wok, add oil. When the oil is hot, add the tofu. Stir-fry 1–2 minutes until golden. Remove tofu from wok, then add broccoli. Stir-fry blanched broccoli 2 minutes.

Mix cornstarch and water together till smooth. Add marinade and cornstarch mixture to wok. Stir to coat. Return tofu to wok and add sesame seeds.

Lamb Stir-Fry

Serves 2

I resist giving you lamb recipes because it is difficult to buy small amounts of tender lamb for stir-frying. My butcher recommends a boned leg of lamb, cut into ½- to 1-pound pieces that you wrap and freeze for use at a later date.

Marinade:

1 tablespoon oil
1 tablespoon sherry
1 tablespoon soy sauce
¼ teaspoon crushed Szechuan peppercorns

1 pound lamb, cut thinly against the grain

Sauce:

2 teaspoons rice vinegar
1 teaspoon sesame oil
1 teaspoon soy sauce
2 teaspoons cornstarch

2 tablespoons oil
2 teaspoons garlic
4 scallions, sliced on the diagonal in 1-inch lengths
6 cups raw spinach leaves, blanched for 30 seconds and chopped coarsely

Combine ingredients for marinade. Add lamb and let stand 15 minutes.

Combine sauce ingredients and set aside.

Heat wok, add oil. When oil is hot, add 2 tablespoons sauce mixture. Add garlic, then lamb. Cook 3–4 minutes until lamb is just browned. Add scallions and spinach. Clear the center of the wok. Pour in sauce. Bring to a boil. Stir to coat. Cook to heat scallions through.

Vegetable Stir-Fry

Serves 2

A simple stir-fry of readily available ingredients.

Sauce:

2 teaspoons soy sauce
1 teaspoon sherry
½ teaspoon sugar
1 teaspoon cornstarch
¼ teaspoon sesame oil

2 tablespoons oil
1 teaspoon minced garlic
1 teaspoon minced ginger
1 large onion, thinly sliced
1 green pepper, seeded and sliced ½ inch wide
1 red pepper, seeded and sliced ½ inch wide
2 8-×-1½-inch zucchini, cut in large julienne strips

Combine sauce ingredients and set aside.

Heat wok. When the wok is hot, add oil. Add garlic and ginger, stir 10 seconds, then add the onion. Stir-fry 1 minute, then add peppers and zucchini. Stir-fry 2–3 minutes. Add sauce and stir to coat.

Teriyaki Stir-Fried Chicken and Shrimp

Serves 2

½ cup teriyaki sauce
1 boneless chicken breast, cut in 1-inch dice
½ pound shrimp, peeled and deveined
1 tablespoon cornstarch
2 tablespoons oil
1 carrot, thinly sliced and blanched for 5 minutes
½ cup bamboo shoots
½ cup peas

Combine teriyaki sauce with chicken and shrimp. Let stand for at least an hour.

Drain chicken and shrimp, reserve marinade. Add cornstarch to marinade. Heat wok. When the wok is hot, add oil. When oil is hot, add chicken and shrimp. Stir-fry 2 minutes. Add carrot and stir-fry 1 minute. Add bamboo shoots and peas, then add reserved marinade. Stir to coat; cook until bamboo shoots are heated through and sauce thickens.

Oriental Sloppy Joes

Serves 2 hearty appetites

Sauce:
½ cup Hoisin sauce
¼ cup chicken broth
2 tablespoons ketchup
2 tablespoons soy sauce

1 tablespoon oil
2 teaspoons minced garlic
2 tablespoons minced onion
2 tablespoons minced green *or* red pepper
½ pound ground pork
1 teaspoon sugar
¼ cup crumbled peanuts
2 rolls
Lettuce

Combine sauce ingredients. Set aside.

Heat wok. When the wok is hot, add oil, and when the oil is hot, add the garlic and onion. Stir to flavor oil, then add pepper and pork. Stir-fry until pork is no longer pink.

Pour off any excess fat. Add the sauce mixture and sugar. Stir to blend. Simmer 5 minutes. Stir in peanuts. Serve on rolls with lettuce.

Sesame Beef with Watercress

Serves 2

½ pound beef, sliced thinly against the grain

Marinade:
2 teaspoons soy sauce
1 teaspoon water
1 teaspoon rice wine
½ teaspoon cornstarch

2 tablespoons oil
1 green onion, minced
½ teaspoon ginger, chopped
½ teaspoon garlic, chopped
2 tablespoons soy sauce
2 tablespoons water
1 teaspoon sesame oil
½ teaspoon sugar
1 tablespoon sesame seeds
¾ pound watercress, blanched for 1 minute

Combine beef and marinade; let sit for at least a half hour.

Heat wok. Add 1 tablespoon oil to wok; when oil is hot, add beef and brown 1 minute. Remove from wok.

Add second tablespoon oil and when the oil is hot, add the green onion, ginger, and garlic. Stir-fry 30 seconds, then add the soy sauce, water, sesame oil, and sugar. Bring to a boil, then return the beef to the wok and add sesame seeds. Cook over a high heat until liquid evaporates.

Serve on a bed of watercress.

Spicy Chicken with Peanuts

Serves 4

Marinade:
2 teaspoons soy sauce
1 teaspoon cornstarch
¼ teaspoon sugar
1 teaspoon rice wine

2 chicken breasts, cut in 1-inch dice
3 tablespoons oil
1 cup peanuts, skinless
3 dried red chilies
1 teaspoon minced garlic
1 teaspoon minced ginger
1 chopped jalapeño
8 Chinese dried mushrooms, soaked in hot water for 20 minutes and sliced thinly
½ cup minced scallions
½ teaspoon vinegar
1 teaspoon sesame oil

Combine marinade ingredients. Marinate chicken for 15 minutes.

Heat wok. Add oil to wok. When the oil is hot, add peanuts and cook until just turning brown. Remove peanuts from wok with a slotted spoon. Add red chilies, garlic, and ginger to wok. Remove garlic before the chilies are done, letting the garlic cook for 1 minute. When chilies are browned, discard chilies and garlic. Add chicken to wok and stir-fry 2 minutes. Add jalapeño, mushrooms, and scallions to wok and stir-fry 1 minute more. Return peanuts to wok. Add vinegar and sesame oil and serve.

Clams in Black Bean Sauce

Serves 4 as an appetizer

1 tablespoon oil
1 shallot, minced (about 1 tablespoon)
2 garlic cloves, sliced thinly
1 teaspoon ginger, finely minced
1 cup rice wine
2 tablespoons fermented black beans, rinsed and soaked in water for at least an hour
2 pounds clams (razor, steamer, *or* littleneck)

Heat oil in wok. Reduce heat to medium-low and add shallot and garlic. Cook slowly until translucent. Add ginger, wine, and drained black beans. Bring to a boil, reduce heat to low, and add clams. Cover and cook until clams open, about 5 minutes.

Tex-Mex Stir-Fry

Serves 4

This dish is prepared just like the Oriental stir-fries, but the flavor is Mexican. Serve with rice or in flour tortillas.

Sauce:

½ teaspoon cumin
¼ teaspoon Tabasco sauce
¼ teaspoon oregano
1 tablespoon Chinese parsley, minced (cilantro)
⅛ teaspoon salt
2 teaspoons cornstarch
2 tablespoons tomato juice

2 tablespoons oil
1 teaspoon garlic
1 onion, cut in half, then sliced thinly
1 sweet red pepper, seeded, cut in ½-inch-wide slices
½ pound beef, sliced thinly
¾ cup corn
1 jalapeño, minced
½ cup diced tomato
½ cup cooked kidney beans

Combine sauce ingredients. Set aside.

Heat wok, add oil. When the oil is hot, add the garlic. Give the garlic a stir, then add the onion and pepper. Stir-fry 3–4 minutes until tender. Remove from wok.

Add beef to wok and brown quickly on both sides about 2 minutes. Add corn, jalapeño, and tomato and cook 1 minute more. Return pepper and onion to the wok, stir, then add sauce. Stir to coat and let sauce thicken, about 1 minute. While sauce is thickening, add cooked beans and heat through.

Steaming

Steaming has many uses. I use steaming to heap up leftovers by putting the plate of leftovers right on the steamer rack. Best of all, steaming is the only way I know to revive dried-out rice and stale bread or muffins.

Steaming foods is one of the cleanest cooking methods; the food has no sauce, loses none of its nutrients, and its flavor is simply what was in the food to begin with. Boring? It can sound boring, but many foods have enough flavor on their own, like carrots or onions. There is a school of thought that believes your taste buds become more sensitive and more appreciative when you offer those taste buds simple, unsauced, unseasoned foods (the more you eat steamed foods, the more you'll like them, and the more you'll be able to appreciate their subtle flavors). I recommend experimenting with steaming vegetables, such as broccoli, as a side dish for dinner, rather than simmering those same vegetables in water. The recipe: Steam vegetables over water until tender, and serve.

There are ways to impart flavor to steamed foods, while adding a minimum of calories. Steam over stock, wine, or beer instead of water. Use the water from reconstituting mushrooms for steaming. Toss fish, shellfish, or chicken with herbs, then steam.

Steaming is an effective way of cooking food to retain moisture. Seasonings and flavors added to food will not be diluted when steamed.

This chapter also includes steamed puddings and cakes. The ring pan I have doesn't fit on my steamer rack. I sit the ring pan directly in the water. The ring pan is also too tall, so the wok lid doesn't fit securely. I seal the space with a length of aluminum foil folded in half and wrapped around the space between the lid and the wok. I have steamed in cake layer pans, ring pans, and shallow bowls. The ring pan is the most efficient because steam can circulate from the center as well as the sides. In other words, even if you have to make do with a pan that doesn't fit perfectly, the recipe will still work.

Steamed Mussel Halves with Saffron, Leek, and Tomato

Serves 4 as an appetizer

Steamed or poached mussels are one of my favorite things. Mussels are very inexpensive, and they are fast and easy to cook. I like to remove cooked mussels from their shells and add them to salads or serve piping hot bowls of freshly cooked mussels with some crusty bread as a light supper or appetizer.

1 tablespoon butter
½ cup finely chopped leek
2 teaspoons minced garlic
1 cup white wine
¼ cup cream
2 teaspoons minced parsley

2 teaspoons lemon juice
½ teaspoon saffron threads
¼ cup tomato, seeded and chopped
Salt to taste
Pepper to taste
1½ pounds mussels

Melt butter in wok. Add leeks and garlic and cook until they begin to soften, about 3 minutes. Add ½ cup wine, increase the heat to medium-high, and boil until liquid is reduced by half, about 5 minutes. Add cream, parsley, lemon juice, saffron, and tomato and cook 1 more minute, stirring constantly. Season lightly with salt and pepper. Remove sauce from pan and set aside.

Don't clean the wok at this point. Add ½ cup water and ½ cup white wine to the wok. Bring to a boil. Steam mussels on rack above liquid until just opened, about 5 minutes. Remove mussels from the wok. Remove one half of each mussel shell. Place the mussels in a single layer on steamer racks and top with ½ teaspoon of the sauce. Steam until heated through and serve on trays as an hors d'oeuvres or divided onto plates as an appetizer.

The sauce and mussels can be made in advance and then combined and given their final steaming right before serving.

Steamed Striped Bass

Serves 2

½ cup water
½ cup dry white wine
1 tablespoon mustard powder
½ tablespoon minced garlic
1 tablespoon minced fresh ginger
1 small tomato, diced
1 scallion, diced
1 striped bass, cleaned and cut open

Place water, wine, mustard, garlic, and ginger in the wok and bring to a boil.

Place tomato and scallion inside the bass.

Steam bass above broth until cooked through and flaky.

Variation:
With a sauce—When fish is done, remove from wok and keep warm in the oven. Add 1 tablespoon cornstarch to broth in wok. Cook until sauce thickens and pour over fish.

Steamed Whole Fish

One advantage of steaming is that you won't dry the fish out if it is overcooked a minute, as you would with baking or broiling.

1–2 pounds fish (such as sea bass or snapper), cleaned
2 very thin slices of ginger, cut in half
1 clove of garlic, thinly sliced
1 scallion, cut lengthwise, then into 1-inch segments
2 tablespoons white wine

Cut several gashes about ½ inch deep into the flesh of the fish on both sides. Place ginger, garlic, and scallion in the wine and toss. Place a piece of scallion and a piece of ginger or garlic in each gash. Steam above water until cooked through, 10–15 minutes.

Top fish with a splash of soy sauce and sesame oil and serve.

Steamed Chicken with Dried Mushrooms and Shrimp

Serves 3

Marinade:
1 tablespoon soy sauce
2 teaspoons sherry
1 teaspoon brown sugar
1 teaspoon cornstarch
1 teaspoon minced ginger
1 teaspoon minced garlic

1 boneless chicken breast, cut in 1-inch-wide fingers
8 dried shiitake mushrooms, soaked in water (save the water), then sliced
1 cup Chinese cabbage, shredded
1 tablespoon dried baby shrimp

Combine marinade ingredients in a large, flat bowl. Toss chicken in marinade. Let sit 15 minutes.

Heat mushroom water in wok, about 2 cups in total. Add mushrooms, cabbage, and shrimp to chicken in marinade and toss. Remove chicken, mushrooms, cabbage, and shrimp from marinade and steam, covered, for 30 minutes and serve.

Steamed Shrimp

Serves 2–3

1 pound shrimp, peeled and deveined
2 tablespoons sherry
1 tablespoon soy sauce

Toss the shrimp with the sherry and soy sauce. Steam over water until opaque and curled.

Variation:
Serve on a bed of spinach steamed on another tier of your bamboo steamer.

Steamed Whole Chicken

2 tablespoons sherry
1 tablespoon soy sauce
1 teaspoon salt
1 teaspoon sesame oil
1 teaspoon cornstarch
1 3-pound chicken
3 cups water or chicken broth

Combine sherry, soy sauce, salt, sesame oil, and cornstarch. Rub chicken with mixture. Let sit for 1 hour.

Steam over water or chicken broth until tender, about 40 minutes.

Steamed Duck

1 tablespoon soy sauce
1 tablespoon plum sauce
1 tablespoon Oyster Sauce (see page 37)
2 teaspoons honey
½ teaspoon Tabasco sauce
1 duck
1 teaspoon Five-Spice Powder (see page 36)
1 teaspoon salt

Combine soy sauce, plum sauce, oyster sauce, honey, and Tabasco. Coat the outside of the duck with the sauce mixture.

Combine five-spice powder and salt. Rub the inside of the duck with this mixture.

Steam duck in steamer placed in wok. Steam for 1½ hours until tender.

Use duck in wontons, fried rice, noodle dishes, or shred and serve with black bean sauce.

Black Bean Sauce

1 tablespoon soy sauce
2 teaspoons sherry
1 teaspoon cornstarch
½ teaspoon salt
½ teaspoon sugar
1 teaspoon vinegar
1 tablespoon oil
2 tablespoons Chinese salted black beans, rinsed
2 teaspoons minced garlic

Combine soy sauce, sherry, cornstarch, salt, sugar, and vinegar in a bowl.

Heat the wok, then add the oil. Stir-fry black beans and garlic for thirty seconds. Add the other ingredients to the wok. Stir to blend flavors and serve.

Wontons and Dumplings

I resisted making my own dumplings for a long time. I thought it would be too much work. I was wrong. They are fun and easy to make. My family gobbles them up and praises me between bites. Don't make the same mistake I did—give these recipes a try and then make up your own variations.

These recipes are for small quantities of dumplings to encourage you to make two or three different kinds. When you are making several kinds, one egg will do to seal all of them.

Preparing Wontons or Dumplings

Dice filling ingredients in small pieces. You can use left-overs such as the filling for Picadillo Stuffed Cabbage (page 49) or from stir-fried dishes. For more ideas, see "Left-overs and Mix-and-Match Recipes" on page 191.

Filling and Sealing Wontons

Place a wonton skin on a plate or cutting board with a point facing you. Paint a bit of egg yolk or cornstarch paste (equal parts water and cornstarch) around the edge of the wonton skin. Place about a tablespoon of filling in the middle lower half of the skin. (Use less filling if you want to play with more complicated ways to fold your wontons.) For easy wontons, fold the point away from you down to the point facing you to form a triangle. Pinch the two points together. Now seal the sides of the triangle by pinching or pressing the wonton skin. Join the left and right points of the triangle to each other.

Be prepared for the fact that these tidbits are addicting—no one can eat just one, and I haven't met many people who can stop at four or even five.

Steamed Pork and Shrimp Wontons/Dumplings

Yield: 15 wontons

Filling:
¼ pound ground pork
¼ pound shrimp, peeled, deveined, and diced
¼ cup diced sweet red pepper (about ¼ of a pepper)
½ teaspoon minced garlic
1 tablespoon soy sauce
½ teaspoon sugar

15 wonton skins
1 egg, lightly beaten

Combine filling ingredients. Let sit for 15 minutes to allow flavors to blend.

Fill wontons. (Instructions on how to fill wontons are given on page 97.

Steam wontons for fifteen minutes in a lightly oiled heat-proof dish.

Beef and Szechuan Preserved Vegetable Wontons

Yield: 15 wontons

1 teaspoon cornstarch
1 teaspoon sherry
1 teaspoon orange juice
½ teaspoon honey
1 teaspoon soy sauce
¼ pound ground beef
1 tablespoon minced Szechuan preserved vegetable
1 scallion, minced
3 black mushrooms, soaked in hot water for 20 minutes, then drained and minced
15 wonton skins
1 egg, lightly beaten

Combine cornstarch, sherry, orange juice, honey, and soy sauce. Stir to dissolve cornstarch. Add beef, preserved vegetable, scallion, and mushrooms.

Fill wontons. (Instructions on how to fill wontons are on page 97.) Steam 20 minutes.

Boiled Pork and Mushroom Wontons

Yield: 15 wontons

¼ pound ground pork
⅓ cup diced mushrooms
½ cup minced bok choy
½ tablespoon soy sauce
½ tablespoon sherry
1 teaspoon minced Chinese parsley (cilantro)
15 wonton skins
1 lightly beaten egg
½ cup water
1½ cups beef stock

Combine first eight ingredients. Let sit for 15 minutes to allow flavors to blend. Fill wontons (see page 97 for instructions).

Combine water and beef stock in wok. Bring to a boil, reduce heat to a simmer, and add wontons. Don't crowd the wok as wontons will stick to each other. Boil wontons 10 minutes.

Crab and Shrimp Open Dumplings

Yield: 15 dumplings

¼ pound shrimp, peeled, deveined, and minced
¼ cup crabmeat, shredded
1 teaspoon sherry
1 teaspoon sesame oil
½ teaspoon soy sauce
1 tablespoon cornstarch
½ teaspoon minced ginger
1 egg white, lightly beaten
6 water chestnuts, minced
15 wonton skins

Combine shrimp and crab. Place shellfish in a double layer of paper towels and squeeze out excess liquid.

Combine sherry, sesame oil, soy sauce, and cornstarch. Stir to dissolve cornstarch. Add ginger, egg white, water chestnuts, and shellfish.

To fill, place a small amount of the mixture in the center of a wonton skin. Slice off the corners of the wonton skin. Pleat the edge of the wonton skin until the skin is pulled up around the wonton. There will be a bit of the filling exposed at the top of the dumpling. Steam 20 minutes.

Duck and Cabbage Dumplings

Yield: 15 dumplings

1 cup meat from ½ a Red-Cooked Duck (see recipe on page 114), minced
½ cup shredded cabbage
¼ cup minced scallion
2 tablespoons Plum Sauce (page 37)
1 tablespoon Hoisin sauce
15 wonton skins
1 egg, lightly beaten

Combine ingredients and fill wontons. (Instructions on how to fill wontons are given on page 97.) Steam for 20 minutes.

Bloody Mary Steamed Fish

Serves 2

You don't have to use my Bloody Mary recipe—any Bloody Mary recipe will work. Go light on the spicy heat of the sauce; as it simmers and reduces, it gets hotter.

This dish is a rebellion against my high school home economics teacher. She said never serve fish and cauliflower together because then the dinner is all white. I found a solution to that problem.

Sauce:

1 12-ounce can V-8 juice
1 teaspoon horseradish
1 teaspoon Worcestershire sauce
2 shakes Tabasco sauce
¼ teaspoon celery seed
⅛ teaspoon black pepper
2 teaspoons lemon juice
1 teaspoon capers

2 8-ounce firm fish filets (catfish, weakfish, cod)
2 ¾-cup servings of cauliflower, in large florets

Combine sauce ingredients in wok. Bring to a boil, then reduce to medium heat.

Place fish and cauliflower in steamer over Bloody Mary mix. Steam about 15 minutes, depending on the thickness of the fish, until fish is cooked, but still tender. Remove fish and cauliflower and boil sauce 5 minutes to reduce.

Pour a pool of sauce on each of two plates. Place fish and cauliflower on the sauce, and serve.

Desserts

Leftover Rice Pudding

Serves 4

1 egg
¼ cup sugar
Pinch salt
1½ cups milk
⅛ teaspoon ground nutmeg
⅛ teaspoon ground cloves
1 cup leftover cooked rice

Beat egg slightly. Add sugar, salt, milk, and spices. Stir in rice. Pour into greased heat-proof flat bowl or ring pan. Steam in wok about 1½ hours until custard sets and rice is soft.

Maple Gingerbread

In this recipe the crystallized ginger is tossed with the flour to keep it from sinking to the bottom when cooked. The same applies to nuts and raisins in cake recipes.

2 cups all-purpose flour
1 teaspoon ground ginger
1 teaspoon baking soda
½ teaspoon ground cloves
2 tablespoons candied ginger, minced
¼ cup butter, softened
¼ cup packed brown sugar
2 eggs
½ cup maple syrup
¼ cup milk

Combine flour, ginger, baking soda, and cloves. Stir in candied ginger to coat. In small mixer bowl, beat butter and sugar until light colored. Beat in eggs, one at a time. Combine syrup and milk. Add dry ingredients and syrup mixture alternately to beaten mixture, beating after each addition. Spoon into a greased and floured tube pan.

Steam in wok in boiling water. Water will come about halfway up the side of the pan. Cover and steam 45 minutes until toothpick comes out clean.

Serve warm or cold, or toasted with butter and marmalade.

Steamed Chocolate Cake

6 ounces semisweet chocolate
4 tablespoons butter
⅓ cup sugar
1 egg
2 cups flour
1 tablespoon baking powder
¼ teaspoon salt
½ teaspoon cinnamon
1 cup milk

Melt chocolate and butter in the top of a double boiler, stirring constantly (do not use your wok). Or use a microwave: cook 30 seconds, stir, then cook 30 seconds more; repeat until chocolate is melted.

Beat sugar and melted chocolate mixture together. Beat in egg. Combine dry ingredients. Add milk and flour mixture alternately to chocolate mixture.

Spoon into a greased and floured ring pan. Place pan in wok of boiling water. Steam about 1 hour. Serve alone or on a pool of custard sauce.

Custard Sauce

3 egg yolks
¼ cup sugar
⅛ teaspoon salt
2 cups milk
1 teaspoon vanilla extract

Combine ingredients in the top of a double boiler. Stir constantly until sauce thickens. Remove from the heat when sauce is a good thickness. Sauce will continue to thicken to the consistency of a pudding if cooked longer.

Variations:
Substitute dark rum for the vanilla

Cappuccino Custard Sauce: replace vanilla and 1 cup of the milk with ½ cup of strong, hot black coffee

Side Dishes

Indian Pudding

Serves 6

1 tablespoon butter
4 cups milk
⅓ cup cornmeal
⅔ cup molasses
3 tablespoons brown sugar
¼ teaspoon cinnamon
¼ teaspoon nutmeg
½ teaspoon powdered ginger
½ teaspoon salt
1 beaten egg
1 apple, cut in ¼-inch-thick slices
3 cups boiling water

Butter a ring pan.

Heat milk until it just begins to bubble at the edges. Remove ½ cup of the milk and combine it with the cornmeal, then add the milk/cornmeal to the rest of the milk. Whisk in cornmeal. Cook 20 minutes, stirring continuously. The mixture will thicken.

Add molasses, brown sugar, and spices. Stir into the cornmeal mixture. Remove from the heat and add the egg.

Place apples in the pan then pour batter over.

Clean the wok and fill with boiling water.

Steam pudding for 2 hours until set. Add more boiling water as needed.

Crustless Corn Quiche

Serves 4

3 tablespoons butter
¼ cup bread crumbs
¾ cup minced onion
1½ tablespoons flour
⅔ cup milk
3 eggs
2 cups corn kernels
¼ cup minced ham
1 tablespoon sugar
1 teaspoon salt
½ teaspoon pepper
A dash or two of Tabasco sauce
⅛ teaspoon nutmeg
⅔ cup shredded Swiss cheese

Melt 1 tablespoon butter in the wok. Add bread crumbs, cook and stir, about 3 minutes until lightly browned. Set aside.

Wipe the wok out, then melt the other 2 tablespoons butter. Sauté the onion until soft. Add flour and milk and stir. Cook until milk thickens slightly. Add eggs, then corn and ham, stirring as you add each ingredient. Add the rest of the ingredients. Stir to blend.

Pour into cake layer pan or springform pan. Steam over or in water for 30 minutes until set. Sprinkle with bread crumbs and serve.

Variations:
Replace the ham with red pepper and sauté the pepper with the onion.

Add 2 tablespoons minced parsley for color.

Try Cheddar or a smoked cheese instead of Swiss.

Add 2 tablespoons white wine when you add the eggs.

Broccoli Pudding

Serves 4

This steamed pudding is wonderful for breakfast.

Topping:
1 tablespoon butter
¼ cup bread crumbs
2 tablespoons grated Parmesan cheese

2 tablespoons butter
1 Italian or hard roll, torn into very small pieces
⅓ cup milk
3 eggs, room temperature
3 cups small broccoli florets, blanched for 3 minutes
3 tablespoons sour cream
¼ teaspoon salt

Start by taking the butter, eggs, and sour cream out of the refrigerator to soften at room temperature.

To make topping, melt butter in the wok. Add bread crumbs, cook and stir about 3 minutes until lightly browned. Remove from wok and combine with Parmesan. Set aside.

Butter a tube pan using 1 tablespoon butter. Set aside.

Soak roll in milk until soft, about 5 minutes.

Separate eggs. Combine yolks with roll, sour cream, and salt. Beat together until fluffy, about 5 minutes.

Beat egg whites with cleaned, dried beaters until stiff, but not dry.

Add broccoli and ⅓ of the egg whites to the egg yolk mixture. Stir to combine. Fold in the rest of the egg whites and the salt.

Steam above water for 1 hour until set. Remove from the steamer when done. Let sit 10 minutes before unmolding. Garnish with topping.

Ricotta, Spinach, and Beef Pudding

Serves 4 as a light supper

½ teaspoon salt
½ pound ground beef
1 cup ricotta cheese
¼ cup milk
1 egg yolk, lightly beaten
1 cup spinach, lightly steamed or defrosted
½ teaspoon nutmeg
¼ teaspoon pepper
2 tablespoons minced parsley
1 tablespoon butter
½ cup tomato sauce

Heat the wok. Add the salt, then the beef, and brown the beef. When the beef is browned, remove it from the wok. Wipe the wok out.

Combine the ricotta, milk, and the egg yolk. Stir in the nutmeg, pepper, and parsley.

Butter a pan. Layer first one-third of the ricotta mixture then combine the rest of the ricotta mixture with the beef and the spinach. Drizzle the tomato sauce over the top. The sauce will be a thin layer. Steam for ½ hour over boiling water in the wok.

Poach and Simmer

What I like about poaching is that the liquid that results can be used as stock. Don't waste it.

Poaching is similar to steaming, but the cooking liquid is integral to the dish. The flavors of the broth permeate the food, and the food flavors the broth.

Simmering is used for stews. Simmering is used in some Chinese dishes, but is much more common in Western cooking. Paella (page 51), Beef Stew with Red Wine (page 53), and Picadillo Stuffed Cabbage (page 49) in the "Classics" chapter are examples of simmered dishes.

Red-Cooked Duck

Serves 3

Cook duck one day ahead. Red-cooked refers to the soy sauce that colors the meat.

½ cup soy sauce
½ cup sherry
1 duck
1 teaspoon Five-Spice Powder (see recipe on page 36)
2 quarter-sized slices of ginger
1 teaspoon honey
2 teaspoons cornstarch
1 tablespoon cold water

Heat wok. Add soy sauce and sherry, and bring to a boil. Add duck and cook, turning the duck to brown each side. Remove duck and rub five spice powder into the skin. Add ginger and honey to wok, then add duck. Fill wok halfway with water and bring to a boil. Reduce heat to low, cover, and simmer 1 hour, turning every 15 minutes.

Remove duck from the wok and chill overnight.

Defat the stock in the wok by also chilling it overnight. The fat will rise to the top and can then be spooned off.

Place 1 cup of the duck stock in the wok. Cook 5–7 minutes to reduce slightly. Mix together cornstarch and water to make a smooth paste. Add it to the stock. Stir to thicken. If lumps appear, strain the gravy.

Slice the duck and steam to warm. Serve duck with steamed vegetables and duck gravy.

Another Red-Cooked Duck Recipe

½ cup soy sauce
¼ cup sherry
1 duck
1 clove of garlic, cut in half
1 teaspoon sugar
1 piece dried tangerine peel
1 onion, thinly sliced
2 teaspoons cornstarch
1 tablespoon water

Heat wok. Add soy sauce and sherry, and bring to a boil. Add duck and cook, turning the duck to brown each side. Remove duck when browned. Add garlic and sugar to the wok, fill wok halfway with water and bring to a boil. Return duck to the wok, and add tangerine peel and onion. Reduce heat to low, cover, and simmer 1 hour, turning every 15 minutes.

Remove duck from the wok. Remove the tangerine peel from the liquid in the wok. Strain onions from the stock and save. Chill both the duck and the stock separately overnight.

Defat the chilled stock by spooning the fat off the top.

Place 1 cup duck stock in the wok. Cook 5–7 minutes to reduce slightly. Mix together cornstarch and water to make a smooth paste. Add it to the stock. Stir to thicken. If lumps appear, strain the gravy.

Slice the duck and combine duck slices with onions. Steam to warm. Serve duck with steamed onions and duck gravy.

Red-Cooked Pork

This recipe is for use with other dishes.

⅓ cup soy sauce
2 cups water
1 clove of garlic, halved
2 quarter-size slices of ginger
2 tablespoons sherry
1 teaspoon sugar
2 pounds pork butt

Combine all ingredients except pork in wok. Stir to blend. Add pork. Simmer 1 hour. Turn pork butts occasionally.

Remove pork from the wok. Shred the pork when it is cool enough to handle.

Use pork in rice and noodle dishes.

Broth Fondue

Serves 4

1½ pounds thinly sliced raw beef and/or chicken
½ head Chinese cabbage (each leaf cut in quarters)
1 pound spinach, stems removed

Broth:
3 cups chicken stock
1 teaspoon minced garlic
1 teaspoon minced ginger
¼ cup soy sauce
2 tablespoons sherry
A dash of sesame oil
2 ounces bean thread noodles (blanched 10 minutes)

Arrange beef and/or chicken meat and vegetables on plate.

Combine broth ingredients in wok and bring to a boil, then reduce heat to a simmer. Serve in an electric wok so the broth stays hot or in a regular wok on a portable electric burner.

Dip meat and vegetables in the simmering broth until cooked, about 2 minutes.

Finish the meal by adding the noodles to the broth that the meat was cooked in. Divide into bowls and serve.

Seafood Fondue

Serves 4

1½ cups stock (fish, chicken, *or* vegetable)
2 tablespoons Hoisin sauce
2 tablespoons rice wine vinegar
2 teaspoons brown sugar
1 tablespoon soy sauce
1 tablespoon minced ginger
¼ teaspoon red pepper flakes
¼ teaspoon sesame oil
1½ pounds shrimp
½ head Chinese cabbage (each leaf cut in quarters)
1 pound spinach, stems removed
2 ounces bean thread noodles (blanched 10 minutes)

Combine the first 8 ingredients. Add the shrimp and let sit for 1 hour.

Strain liquid into wok. Heat to a boil. Serve in an electric wok so the broth stays hot or in a regular wok on a portable electric burner.

Dip shrimp and vegetables in the simmering broth until cooked, about 2 minutes.

Finish the meal by adding the noodles to the broth that the food was cooked in. Divide into bowls and serve.

Poached Chicken

- 1 3-pound chicken, cut in 8 pieces
- 2 leeks, washed and cut in 2-inch pieces
- 1 clove of garlic, cut in half
- 1 onion, quartered
- 3 stalks of celery, cut in 2-inch pieces
- 3 carrots, washed and cut in 2-inch pieces
- 4 sprigs of parsley
- 1 teaspoon dried thyme
- 1 bay leaf
- ½ teaspoon salt
- 6 whole peppercorns
- Water
- 2 tablespoons butter
- 4 tablespoons flour
- 1 cup half-and-half
- ¼ teaspoon ground nutmeg
- Dash of Tabasco sauce
- 2 tablespoons lemon juice

Place chicken in wok with the leeks, garlic, onion, celery, carrots, parsley, thyme, bay leaf, salt, and pepper. Cover with water. Bring to a boil, reduce heat, and cover. Simmer for about 45 minutes until the chicken is tender and cooked through. Skim fat occasionally.

Remove chicken and carrots from the wok and keep warm in a covered dish. Strain the stock and discard the herbs and other vegetables.

Melt butter in the wok. Add flour and stir over a low heat until flour is lightly browned. Add two cups of the stock. (Freeze leftover stock for use in the future.) Stir to blend with the flour. Bring to a boil and cook for 10 minutes, stirring. The stock will thicken slightly.

Add half-and-half, nutmeg, Tabasco, and lemon juice. Simmer and stir for 5 minutes.

Serve with rice, noodles, or potatoes.

Simmered Chicken Wings

Serves 4 as a first course

16 chicken wings
3 tablespoons oil
¼ cup soy sauce
¼ cup sherry
½ cup water
1 tablespoon brown sugar
1 tablespoon sesame oil
2 tablespoons sesame seeds
1 teaspoon minced garlic

Brown wings in oil, remove, then drain off excess oil.

Place all remaining ingredients in wok and stir to blend flavors. Add chicken wings and bring to a boil, then reduce heat and simmer, covered, for 30 minutes. Stir occasionally.

Uncover pan and simmer 15 minutes more, stirring frequently to keep from sticking.

Poached Salmon with Mushrooms and Cream

Serves 4

Butter will burn much more easily than the oil used in Chinese wok cooking, so when sautéing with butter, set the stove no higher than medium. This recipe begins with a classic French sauce called Beurre Blanc. Stir it with a whisk for easy mixing.

Beurre Blanc with Cream:

3 tablespoons butter, softened
2 shallots, finely chopped
½ cup dry white wine
¼ teaspoon ground white pepper
1 cup heavy cream

1 tablespoon butter
6–7 mushrooms, sliced
3 cups water
1 medium onion, quartered
2 carrots, cut in 1-inch pieces
2 celery stalks, cut in 1-inch pieces
1 bay leaf
¼ teaspoon thyme
6 whole peppercorns
½ cup wine
1 tablespoon lemon juice
4 salmon fillets, 6–8 ounces each

Heat 1 tablespoon butter in wok over a medium-low heat until melted. Add shallots and sauté until softened. Add wine and pepper. Raise heat and boil until reduced to half its original volume. Lower heat to a simmer, and add cream. Stir until sauce is well combined and thickened, about 7–10 minutes. Remove from the heat and stir in 2 tablespoons butter, adding ½ tablespoon at a time. If the butter is not mixing and melting in, return to the stove over a very low heat. Pour sauce out of the wok and set aside.

Reheat wok. Add 1 tablespoon butter and sauté mushrooms over a medium heat for about 5 minutes, until the mushrooms have released their liquid and that liquid has cooked off. Add mushrooms to the Beurre Blanc.

Place water, onion, carrots, celery, and seasonings in the wok. Bring to a boil. Allow to boil for 30 minutes. Add wine and lemon juice and boil 30 minutes more. Next, steam salmon fillets about 6–8 minutes until cooked through. The liquid left in the wok is a fish stock. Freeze the fish stock for use at a later date.

Winter Wine-Poached Pear Compote

Serves 4

1 cup red wine
1 cup water
¼ cup sugar
1 teaspoon vanilla extract
8 dried apricots
8 prunes, pitted
4 pears, peeled and halved

Combine red wine, water, and sugar in the wok. Bring to a boil and cook 10 minutes. Add vanilla and the dried fruit and cook 10 minutes in the liquid. Add the pears and cook 10 minutes more until tender.

Oyster and Spinach Stuffed Sea Bass

Serves 4

This dish is similar to steamed fish, but without the need of a steamer. The fish is poached in a small amount of seasoned liquid.

1 pinch nutmeg
¼ teaspoon minced fresh ginger
½ teaspoon sesame oil
1 cup spinach, steamed or defrosted
1 1½-pound sea bass, split, with bones removed
Salt
6 oysters, removed from shell
1 tablespoon chopped scallion
2 tablespoons sherry
½ cup water
1 teaspoon soy sauce

Toss nutmeg, ginger, and sesame oil with spinach.

Pat sea bass inside and out to wipe off excess moisture. Salt lightly. Open sea bass and place oysters inside. Top with spinach mixture and then sprinkle with scallions.

Add sherry, water, and soy sauce to wok. Heat over medium heat for 1 minute. Place whole fish gently in wok. Cook, covered, over medium to low flame until fish is opaque and flaky, approximately 15–20 minutes.

Wok Frying

My first thought about frying is whether you'll actually try these recipes. Everyone loves fried foods, but the nutritionists have scared us off. When food is correctly deep-fried, the flavor is sealed in and the coating is golden and crunchy. Food will not taste oily. Think about French fries. There really is nothing that tastes quite the same when they are done right. Give deep-frying a try—it's worth it.

Frying in a wok is better than in other pans because the shape of the wok allows you achieve a greater depth of oil using less of it than if you were cooking in a straight-sided pan. Three cups of oil will usually be enough to achieve a depth of two inches. No more than that is needed. Because oil can bubble and splatter, it needs room to do that *within* the wok. Remember that the level of the oil will rise as the oil heats and expands. The level of the oil will also rise when food is added.

Caution

Hot oil can cause very bad burns, so be careful. Be especially careful to turn the long handle of a wok away from where it can be hit by someone walking by. Also, liquid from marinades or moist fruit in fritters will boil and splatter.

How to Know When the Oil Is Hot

To test to see if the oil is hot enough for frying, drop a pinch of flour in. If it doesn't sizzle, the oil is not hot enough. The flour should sizzle and disappear.

Another way to test the oil is to drop in a cube of bread. The oil should bubble around the edge of the bread and in about thirty to forty seconds the bread will have browned a bit.

You can burn oil, so at the point when the oil appears hot enough, I turn the heat down just a notch, before beginning to cook. Don't cook too much food at once in the oil; it will bring the temperature of the oil down.

Many people use thermometers to judge the correct temperature of oil for frying. If you choose to use a thermometer, the best temperature is between 350° and 400°; 375° is ideal.

The oil should never be heated to the point of smoking. If you let the oil get hot enough to smoke, it will burn and be no good for frying. Burnt oil will make the food taste burnt and bitter.

After you have heated the oil, your next challenge is to keep the oil at a good temperature while cooking. The temperature needs to be monitored constantly. Watch to see if the food is browning too slowly or too quickly, and adjust the heat accordingly.

Other Frying Tips

It is best to fry foods when they are cold. Always give batters time to chill before using.

Foam and debris will form in the oil if you do a lot of frying. Skim off any foam or debris as you go.

Place fried foods on paper towels when done, to drain off excess oil.

Serve savory fried foods on finely chopped lettuce or deep-fried rice noodles. The oil drips down through the lettuce or noodles and away from the fried foods.

Let frying oil cool after using. You can then save the oil to use again, but first strain cooled oil. The oil should still be light and clear, otherwise it's not good for reuse. I use the age-old method of storing oil in a metal coffee can.

Coatings for Frying

In the introduction, I discussed how moisture is the enemy of frying (oil and water don't mix). Foods are coated to give them a dry surface for frying. Cornstarch or flour are the simplest types of coatings. There are wet coatings as well, such as batters or egg.

Twice Frying

Twice frying is exactly what it sounds like. Food is fried for a minute, cooled, and then fried again. Twice frying is how the best French fries are made tender inside and crisp on the outside. If you do not have the patience for frying foods twice, then when the oil acclimates to the food added and is hot again, reduce the heat slightly to keep the outside from burning before the inside is cooked through. Use twice frying if the food is getting dark too quickly. Twice frying is useful and effective for most fried foods.

Fried Foods

Chips

This is the simplest type of frying. No coating or batter is necessary, just plain vegetables fried to a delicious crispness.

Batter-Dipped or Coated Foods

This includes tempura, as well as several other types of batters. The simplest coating is flour.

Fritters

There are two types of fritters. One type is batter-dipped; the other consists of stirring the "filling" into the batter.

Fried Dumplings and Stuffed or Plain Fried Doughs

These recipes require two recipes, one for the dough and another for the filling.

All of the dumplings and wontons that are in the chapter "Steaming" on page 89 can be fried.

Doughnuts, plain or filled, are fried doughs.

Dipping Sauces

There are a variety of sauces for dipping fried foods included in this book. You can even use the left-over sauce to dress salads or in stir-fried dishes.

Deep-Fried Chicken with Sesame Seed Sauce

Serves 4–6

Marinade:

½ teaspoon salt
½ teaspoon sugar
¼ teaspoon pepper
2 teaspoons minced ginger
1 teaspoon minced garlic
2 tablespoons brandy
1 tablespoon soy sauce

1 chicken, cut in 8 pieces
3 cups oil
2 cups cornstarch

Combine ingredients for the marinade. Marinate the chicken for 2 hours.

Heat oil in wok.

Dredge the chicken in cornstarch and deep fry until golden and cooked through, about 15 minutes.

Sesame Seed Sauce

2 tablespoons sesame seeds
2 teaspoons rice wine vinegar
½ cup Hoisin sauce
2 tablespoons honey
2 tablespoons sherry
2 finely minced scallions

Toast sesame seeds in a dry wok over medium heat, taking care not to burn the sesame seeds. Remove seeds and let them cool. Combine other ingredients in wok, then stir in sesame seeds.

Drizzle over chicken.

Deep-Fried Beef with Orange Sauce

Serves 3

3 cups oil
1 egg
1 teaspoon minced garlic
1 cup cornstarch
½ teaspoon salt
1 pound beef, cut in 1-inch cubes

Heat oil in wok.

Combine egg and garlic. Combine cornstarch and salt. Dip beef in egg mixture, then in cornstarch.

Deep-fry beef cubes in oil until golden.

Orange Sauce

2 teaspoons cornstarch
2 tablespoons water
2 teaspoons soy sauce
½ cup orange juice
2 tablespoons sugar
1 tablespoon brandy
¼ cup vinegar

Combine cornstarch, water, and soy sauce. Set aside.

Heat orange juice with sugar and brandy until sugar is dissolved, then add the vinegar. Stir in the cornstarch paste. The sauce will bubble a bit, then thicken. When the sauce has begun to thicken, remove it from the heat and continue to stir for a minute.

Serve beef with orange sauce.

Fried Chicken Wings

Serves 4

3 cups oil
1½ cups cornstarch
¼ teaspoon salt
⅛ teaspoon cayenne pepper
⅛ teaspoon black pepper
2 dozen chicken wings
2 eggs, lightly beaten

Heat oil in wok.

Combine cornstarch and spices. Dip chicken wings in egg, then cornstarch mixture.

Deep-fry wings until golden, about 5 minutes. Serve with a variety of dipping sauces.

Beer Batter Shrimp with Almonds

Serves 3

2 cups oil
1 egg
4 tablespoons flour
½ teaspoon salt
3 tablespoons beer
¼ cup finely chopped almonds
1 pound shrimp, peeled and deveined, leave the tails on

Heat oil in wok.

Combine egg, flour, and salt. Stir in beer, then stir in the almonds.

Dip the shrimp in the batter and fry in batches until golden. Turn down the temperature of the oil slightly after adding the shrimp.

Tempura

2 eggs, separated
1 cup flour
4 tablespoons cornstarch
¾ teaspoon salt
1 teaspoon pepper
1 cup water

In a small bowl, beat egg whites until stiff peaks form. Combine flour, cornstarch, salt, and pepper. Beat egg yolk and water together until frothy and bright. Add flour mixture to egg yolk mixture slowly, and continue beating the mixture. Beat until smooth. Fold in egg white.

Now that the batter is made, you can make tempura with practically anything.

To fry, heat two cups of frying oil in wok until hot. A pinch of flour will sizzle when dropped in hot oil. Do not let the oil boil.

Add about three pieces of tempura to the oil, wait 30 seconds, then add 3 more. Do not overcrowd the pan. Fry until golden: 1–3 minutes for soft, fast-cooking foods like shrimp, zucchini, and mushrooms, and 3–5 minutes for harder foods like carrots and potatoes.

Sweet Potato and Chicken Tempura

Serves 4

4 sweet potatoes, halved, then sliced in ¼-inch slices
2 boneless chicken breasts, sliced in 1-×-3-inch fingers and steamed in the wok until just opaque

Prepare batter and fry as described in tempura recipe on page 130. Serve with lemon wedges or Curried Dipping Sauce (see below).

Curried Dipping Sauce

Yield: ¼ cup sauce

1 teaspoon oil
1 teaspoon minced garlic
1 teaspoon curry powder
2 teaspoons honey
4 tablespoons rice wine vinegar
1 tablespoon lemon juice
2 teaspoons soy sauce
½ teaspoon sesame oil

Heat wok, add oil. When oil is hot, add garlic and curry powder. Stir-fry 30 seconds. Reduce heat to low and add the rest of the ingredients and stir to dissolve honey. Pour into a small, shallow dish and let cool before serving.

Shrimp and Broccoli Tempura

Serves 4

1 pound shrimp, peeled and deveined, leave the tails on
2 cups broccoli florets

Prepare batter and fry as described in tempura recipe on page 130. Serve with Szechuan Dipping Sauce (see below).

Szechuan Dipping Sauce

Yield: ⅓ cup

1 teaspoon minced garlic
1 tablespoon minced ginger
2 tablespoons sesame paste (tahini)
1 tablespoon chili oil
1 tablespoon soy sauce
1 tablespoon sesame oil
1 teaspoon sugar
1 teaspoon rice wine vinegar
⅛ teaspoon ground Szechuan peppercorns

Combine ingredients and let flavors blend overnight before serving.

Vegetarian Tempura

Allow about 1 cup of raw vegetables per person.

Carrots, cut on the diagonal in ¼-inch-thick slices, blanched for 5 minutes
Zucchini, cut on the diagonal in ¼-inch slices
Eggplant, cut in ½-inch-thick slices
Mushrooms, halved
Peppers, cut in 1-inch-wide strips

Prepare batter and fry as described in tempura recipe on page 130. Serve with a variety of dipping sauces.

Beer Batter Vegetable Tempura

Serves 2–3

½ cup flour
½ cup beer
About 2 dozen vegetable pieces (broccoli, cauliflower florets, ½-inch-thick slices of sweet potato, halved mushrooms, onion rings)
3 cups oil

Combine flour and beer. Whisk until smooth. Let sit for a half hour in the refrigerator.

Dip vegetables in batter and fry 1–2 minutes until golden brown.

Serve with a dipping sauce.

Deep-Fried Fish with Julienne Vegetables

Serves 4

Sauce:
2 tablespoons sherry
2 teaspoons soy sauce
1 tablespoon cornstarch
½ teaspoon sugar
¼ teaspoon sesame oil

1½ tablespoons *plus* 2 cups oil
1 teaspoon minced garlic
1 1-inch-thick segment of ginger, julienned
1 carrot, julienned and blanched for 3 minutes
1 small zucchini, julienned
2 scallions, cut along their length, then cut into 1-inch pieces
1 cup shredded Chinese cabbage
¼ cup enoki mushrooms, rinsed
½ cup flour
¼ teaspoon salt
1 egg, lightly beaten
1 sea bass or snapper, cleaned, wiped dry (about 2 pounds)

Combine sauce ingredients and set aside.

Heat wok. When the wok is hot, add 1½ tablespoons oil. Add garlic and ginger, stir-fry 1 minute. Add carrot, zucchini, scallions, and cabbage, stir-fry 2–3 minutes until tender. Add sauce and stir to coat. Remove from wok and set aside in a warm place. Wipe out wok.

Combine flour and salt on a plate. Coat fish with flour, then egg, then flour again.

Heat 2 cups oil in wok. When the oil is very hot, add fish, fry fish for about 2 minutes, turning the fish so that both sides are crisp, then reduce heat slightly. Cook until crisp on the outside and cooked through, about 8–10 minutes.

Top fish with vegetables and serve.

Fried Wonton Skins

Use as a crisp garnish.

Wonton skins (see page 40 for wonton recipe), sliced in ¼–½-inch-wide strips
2 cups oil

Heat oil in wok. Fry wonton skins until lightly browned.

Pita Chips and Dip

Serves 4–6 as an hors d'oeuvre

2 pita bread rounds
2 cups oil
¼ cup chopped fresh tomato
2 tablespoons minced scallion

Cut each pita bread in six wedge-shaped slices. Separate the top from the bottom on the pita bread pieces.

Heat oil in wok. Fry the pita chips lightly in the wok. They brown easily and quickly. Remove after they brown just a bit on each side.

Arrange on a plate. Top with a scoop of dip (see recipe page 136). Garnish with chopped tomato and minced scallion.

Dip

⅔ cup grated Cheddar cheese
¼ cup mayonnaise
1 teaspoon Worcestershire sauce
Dash or two of Tabasco sauce
Salt to taste
Pepper to taste
¼ teaspoon lemon juice
⅛ teaspoon dry mustard

Mix together and spoon in a mound at the center of the pita chips.

Chips and Simple Fried Foods

A variety of root vegetables can be used:

Potatoes, with or without their skins
Sweet potatoes or yams
Turnips
Beets, sweet and brightly colored
Carrots, sliced on the diagonal for a larger chip

Less common:

Lotus root (it looks like lace when sliced)
Daikon radish

Other simple foods to fry:

Parsley or leeks as a garnish
Whole cloves of garlic to then use as a spread on bread
Cooked noodles as a garnish or use them to make a basket to serve a stir-fry dish

Paper-thin slices will give you crisps with no center, much like a commercial potato chip. Slightly thicker slices, as thick as a ¼ inch, will give you crisp outsides with a bit of tenderness at the center. Experiment with different vegetables and different thicknesses.

Sprinkle the chips with salt or serve with one or more of the dipping sauces described in this chapter.

Hint

Soak starchy root vegetables in water for several hours before frying to remove some of the sticky starch from the vegetables. They will stick less and fry crisper.

Fried Chicken and/or Onions

This is the best and simplest recipe for fried chicken and fried onions I know. The onions are terrific as a garnish, a side dish for hamburgers, or as a party munchie.

The fried chicken is good cold at picnics, or hot for a typical Southern supper with mashed potatoes and collard greens.

The onions and chicken don't have to be cooked together, they just use the same recipe.

Onions, sliced paper thin
or
Chicken, cut into legs, thighs, and breasts for frying

Milk, enough to cover the chicken or onions
Tabasco sauce
Flour seasoned with salt, pepper, and paprika (for color)
Cayenne pepper, optional (if you want it hot)

Place chicken or onions in a bowl. Cover with milk. Add lots of Tabasco, enough to turn the milk a pale pink. Don't worry, it won't make the food hot, just flavorful. Marinate for several hours or overnight.

Place seasoned flour in a flat bowl (I use a pie plate). Add cayenne to the flour, if you wish.

Heat oil in wok.

Shake off excess milk. Dip in flour, and fry in oil until cooked through and golden for the chicken (cut into the chicken if necessary to see if the center is cooked). Fry onions until crisp and lightly golden. Dry on paper towels and serve.

Variations:
Try shrimp or oysters using this same recipe. Marinate 1–3 hours, not overnight.

Corn Fritters

Yield: about 2 dozen

½ cup milk
1 egg
1 cup flour
2 tablespoons cornmeal
1 teaspoon salt
1 teaspoon baking powder
1½ cups corn
⅛ teaspoon black pepper
1 tablespoon minced parsley
½ cup chopped red onion
⅛ teaspoon Tabasco sauce or more, to taste
3 cups oil

Beat together milk and egg in a bowl. Add flour, cornmeal, salt, and baking powder. Mix until smooth. Stir corn, pepper, parsley, onion, and Tabasco into batter.

Heat frying oil in wok. Fry tablespoons of fritter dough in hot oil until golden brown and cooked through, about 3 minutes.

Serve as an appetizer or side dish. Corn fritters go well with salsa or cheese sauce (use the cheese sauce in the Macaroni and Cheese recipe on page 47).

Mushroom Fritters

Yield: about 2 dozen

1 tablespoon butter
¼ teaspoon thyme
2 cups fresh mushrooms
1 tablespoon sherry
3 cups oil
½ cup milk
1 egg
1 cup flour
1 teaspoon dry mustard
¼ teaspoon salt
1 teaspoon baking powder
½ cup minced, smoked cooked ham
½ cup shredded Swiss cheese

Heat the wok. When the wok is hot, add the butter. Stir the thyme into the melted butter over a medium heat, then add the mushrooms. Sauté the mushrooms about 5 minutes. Stir in the sherry. Cook 1 minute more. Remove from the wok. Clean the wok before adding the frying oil.

Combine milk and egg in a bowl. Add flour, dry mustard, salt, and baking powder. Stir until smooth. Stir in the mushrooms, ham, and cheese.

Heat frying oil in wok. Fry tablespoons of fritter dough in hot oil until golden brown and cooked through, about 3 minutes.

Serve fritters with meat and gravy or on their own as an hors d'oeuvre.

Apple and Almond Fritters

Yield: about 2 dozen

½ cup milk
1 egg
1¼ cup flour
¼ cup sugar
¼ teaspoon salt
1 teaspoon baking powder
½ teaspoon cinnamon
½ cup chopped almonds
3 cups oil
3 apples, peeled and cut in ¼-inch-thick slices

Combine milk and egg in a bowl. Beat together, then add flour, sugar, salt, baking powder, and cinnamon. Mix until smooth. Stir in almonds.

Heat frying oil in wok. Dip apple slices in batter (make sure to get both sides). Fry in hot oil until golden brown and cooked through, about 3 minutes.

Serve for dessert with maple syrup or powdered sugar, dip in sour cream, or serve with Apricot Dipping Sauce (see below).

Apricot Dipping Sauce

Yield: ½ cup

½ cup apricot preserves
1 tablespoon lemon juice
1 tablespoon apricot brandy

Combine ingredients. Heat until preserves thin and combine with liquid. Cool slightly and serve.

Cherry Fritters

Yield: about 2 dozen

2 cups frozen, defrosted, *or* fresh pitted cherries
2 tablespoons orange liqueur
½ cup milk
1 egg
1½ cup flour
¼ teaspoon salt
1 teaspoon baking powder
¼ teaspoon nutmeg
3 cups oil

Combine cherries and liqueur. Marinate 1 hour, then drain.

Combine milk and egg in a bowl. Beat together, then add flour, salt, baking powder, and nutmeg. Mix until smooth. Stir in cherries.

Heat frying oil in wok. Fry tablespoons of fritter dough in hot oil until golden brown and cooked through, about 3 minutes.

Serve for dessert with Orange Sauce (see below) or with duck, pork, or turkey dishes.

Orange Sauce

¼ cup orange juice
1 tablespoon lemon juice
2 tablespoons orange marmalade
¼ cup honey

Combine all ingredients and heat in a pan until marmalade and honey dissolve, then simmer until liquid thickens. Let cool slightly before serving.

Spiced Fritters

Yield: about 18

½ cup milk
1 egg
⅓ cup sugar
1 cup flour
¼ teaspoon salt
1 teaspoon baking powder
¼ teaspoon cinnamon
⅛ teaspoon nutmeg
⅛ teaspoon ground clove
Pinch of ground black pepper
3 cups oil

Beat together milk and egg in a bowl. Add sugar, flour, salt, baking powder, and spices. Mix until smooth.

Heat frying oil in wok. Fry tablespoons of fritter dough in hot oil until golden brown and cooked through, about 3 minutes.

Serve for dessert with maple syrup, a fruit sauce (try Apricot Dipping Sauce on page 141, or Orange Sauce on page 142), or fruit compote.

Fried Pâte à Choux (Cream Puff Dough)

½ cup water
½ cup milk
½ cup butter
1 teaspoon sugar
¼ teaspoon salt
1 cup flour
4 eggs
1 teaspoon vanilla *or* almond extract
3 cups oil
Jam or fruit butter
Confectioners' sugar

Combine water, milk, butter, sugar, and salt in a high-sided saucepan. Cook slowly until the butter melts, then allow it to come to a rapid boil (it will look like it will boil over). At that point, and no sooner, add flour all at once. Remove the pot from the heat and stir quickly until dough forms a ball and pulls away from the sides. Place on the heat for 20–30 seconds more.

Remove from heat and stir in eggs one at a time. Add extract.

Heat oil in wok. Deep-fry tablespoons of dough. Puffs are done when golden and light. If the center is not cooked, remove that dough before filling. Fill with jam, dust with confectioners' sugar, and serve.

Variation:

Fill with chilled vanilla custard.

Drizzle with chocolate sauce.

Fill with ice cream and top with chocolate sauce.

Dipping Sauces for Savory Fritters or Tempura

Hoisin and Orange Sauce

Yield: ½ cup

½ cup orange juice
1 tablespoon Hoisin Sauce

Simply stir together, then serve.

Plum Dipping Sauce

Yield: ½ cup

⅓ cup plum sauce (see page 37)
2 tablespoons Hoisin sauce

Stir together and it's ready to serve. Use with Mu Shu dishes.

Sesame Ginger Sauce

Yield: ½ cup

¼ cup sesame paste or tahini
2 tablespoons soy sauce
1 teaspoon sugar
1 teaspoon hot chili oil
1½ tablespoons sesame oil
1½ tablespoons rice wine vinegar
1½ tablespoons rice wine
1 tablespoon finely minced cilantro

Combine ingredients. Serve.

Spicy Honey Dipping Sauce

Yield: ½ cup

¼ teaspoon red pepper flakes
¼ teaspoon Tabasco sauce
1 teaspoon minced garlic
¼ cup honey
3 tablespoons lime juice
1 tablespoon fish sauce

Combine ingredients and heat to blend flavors and dissolve honey. When the ingredients are well-combined, cool and serve.

Pineapple Plum Sauce

Yield: ½ cup

⅓ cup crushed pineapple
3 tablespoons plum sauce
1 teaspoon soy sauce

Combine ingredients and serve.

Leftover Mashed Potato Fritters

Serves 3 as a side dish

2 cups cold leftover mashed potatoes
½ cup flour
¼ cup Parmesan cheese
1 teaspoon thyme
1 egg, lightly beaten
½ cup fine, dry bread crumbs
2 cups oil

Form the mashed potatoes into patties, using about ¼ of a cup of potato per ½-inch-thick patty.

Combine the flour, Parmesan, and thyme. Roll the balls in the flour mixture, then the egg, then the bread crumbs. Chill one hour.

Heat oil in wok. When the oil is hot, add fritters and fry until crisp and brown, about 5 minutes. Drain and serve.

Pumpkin or Applesauce Doughnuts

I divide the dough in two and add a half cup pumpkin to one half and a half cup applesauce to the other. I like having two kinds of doughnuts to serve instead of one. The batter can be made in advance, covered well, and left to rise overnight in the refrigerator. Refrigerating produces even lighter doughnuts. It also prevents having to get up before dawn to start making doughnuts for Sunday brunch.

1 package of yeast
⅛ teaspoon salt
½ cup very hot tap water
2⅓ cups flour
3 eggs
1 tablespoon oil
1 tablespoon dark rum
⅓ cup sugar
1 cup pumpkin puree *and* ½ teaspoon nutmeg
or
1 cup applesauce *and* ½ teaspoon cinnamon
2 cups oil
Confectioners' sugar

Combine yeast, salt, and hot water in a large bowl. Stir to dissolve yeast. Add 1 cup flour and stir until smooth. Let sit in a warm place for 1 hour, or until double in size.

Beat eggs until frothy, add remaining 1⅓ cups flour and oil. Stir until well mixed.

When the dough is done rising, add the egg mixture, rum, sugar, and pumpkin and nutmeg (*or* applesauce and cinnamon) to the dough. Stir to blend. This will require a bit of work as the elastic dough will resist the ingredients added to it. Stir until smooth and well mixed. Let rise in a warm place for 1 hour.

Heat oil in the wok. Fry soup spoonfuls of shaped dough in the hot oil until golden and light. Fry a bit on each side to seal, then finish frying on each side until golden and light, about 2 minutes. Dry on paper towels, and sprinkle with confectioners' sugar.

Coconut Shrimp Balls

Yield: 2 dozen

1 pound shrimp, peeled, deveined, and finely chopped
2 eggs, lightly beaten
1 teaspoon ground coriander
½ teaspoon cumin
¼ teaspoon paprika
⅛ teaspoon cayenne pepper
½ teaspoon salt
¼ cup grated coconut
1 tablespoon cornstarch
¼ cup bread crumbs
3 cups oil

Combine the shrimp, eggs, and spices in a bowl. Stir in the coconut, cornstarch, and bread crumbs. Form walnut-size balls. Do not handle too much.

Heat oil in wok. When the oil is very hot, fry balls in the oil until golden, about 3 minutes. Serve with Fruity Dipping Sauce (see recipe page 150).

Fruity Dipping Sauce

Yield: ½ cup

⅔ cup rice wine
⅓ cup sweet fruit wine (plum, raspberry, *or* blackberry)
¼ teaspoon dry mustard
½ teaspoon minced fresh ginger
3 tablespoons fruit chutney (peach, mango, *or* plum)

Combine wines and boil. Reduce by half (boil away half the liquid). Add the mustard, ginger, and chutney, and simmer until chutney blends with other ingredients and sauce thickens.

Corn and Crab Fritters

Yield: 2 dozen

2 eggs
⅛ teaspoon salt
½ teaspoon baking powder
¼ teaspoon ground sage
3 dashes Tabasco sauce
2 cups corn
2 cups crabmeat
2 minced shallots
2 tablespoons chopped red onion
2 tablespoons chopped parsley
1 tablespoon cornstarch
3 cups oil

Lightly beat eggs in a bowl. Stir in salt, baking powder, sage, and Tabasco. Now stir in the corn, crab, shallots, red onion, and parsley. Sprinkle the cornstarch over and then stir it in.

Heat oil in the wok. Fry tablespoons of dough until golden, about 4 minutes.

Chocolate Kiss Fritters

Serves 8

1 package of refrigerator crescent dough, cut to wonton-size squares
16 chocolate kisses, removed from their wrappers
2 cups oil

Wrap the chocolate kisses in crescent dough. Heat oil in wok. Fry fritters until golden. Eat warm while the chocolate is still melted.

House Specialties

These are the family favorites. They are all made in a wok. Some were developed for the wok, some were adapted for the wok. They are now made in a wok because that is always the first pan I reach for.

When I was over at a neighbor's giving them taste tests of everything from fritters to noodles, they said they had a wok but never used it. In my house it's more likely all the frying pans are never used.

Try making all of your favorites in a wok.

Linguini with Tomato Pesto

Serves 2

I make my own pesto, but there are quality ready-made versions available.

¼ cup white wine
2 large tomatoes, cut in ½-inch chunks
¼ cup pesto
¾ pound linguini, prepared according to package directions

Place the white wine in the wok. Heat to boiling, then reduce heat to medium, and add the tomatoes. Cook just to heat through. Stir in the pesto (see below). Add linguini, toss, and serve.

Pesto

1½ cups basil
½ cup parsley
⅓ cup nuts
⅓ cup oil
2 cloves garlic
½ cup Parmesan cheese

Combine basil, parsley, nuts, oil, and garlic in a blender or food processor. When well mixed, stir in Parmesan cheese.

This recipe makes 2 cups of pesto. The leftover pesto can be frozen or topped with a layer of olive oil and refrigerated.

Barbecue Pork Sandwiches*

Serves 4

2 tablespoons Worcestershire sauce
2 tablespoons soy sauce
4 tablespoons sugar
4 tablespoons vinegar
2 dashes Tabasco sauce
1 cup tomato puree
1 cup water
1 cup minced onion
1½ pounds pork butt
4 hard rolls

Combine first 8 ingredients in your wok, stirring to blend. Add pork and simmer, covered, for 1½ hours. Remove pork and when it is cool enough to handle, shred. Simmer sauce left in the wok for 5 minutes more to thicken. Toss shredded pork with sauce. Serve on rolls.

Variation:
Chop leftover fried onions to use for garnish.

*Leftover pork from this recipe can be used instead of the beef in the Stove-Top Tamale Pie on page 57.

Lamb Meatballs

Serves 4

¼ cup finely chopped onion
2 teaspoons minced garlic
1 tablespoon *plus* ¼ cup oil
1 egg, lightly beaten
1 teaspoon paprika
½ teaspoon dried thyme
½ teaspoon cumin
⅛ teaspoon red pepper flakes
⅛ teaspoon salt
⅛ teaspoon pepper
1 pound lean ground lamb
½ cup dry bread crumbs
2 tablespoons chopped fresh mint
2 tablespoons chopped fresh parsley

Sauté the onion and garlic in 1 tablespoon oil in the wok until they are soft and translucent. Remove from wok and blot away excess oil.

Combine all ingredients including the cooked onions and garlic, but not the remaining oil. Set aside in the refrigerator 15–30 minutes to blend flavors.

Form walnut-sized meatballs. Heat ¼ cup oil in wok until hot. Add meatballs and brown, cooking until done. Do not add too many meatballs at a time to the wok. Drain cooked meatballs on paper towels.

Serve hot on egg noodles with Tomato Cream Sauce (see page 157).

Tomato Cream Sauce

½ cup sherry
¼ cup white wine
3 tablespoons minced shallots
2 cups cream
¼ teaspoon grated lemon peel
1 tablespoon minced fresh mint
1 cup peeled, seeded, chopped tomatoes (blanch tomatoes for 30 seconds to make peeling easy)

Cook sherry and wine with shallots. Simmer until reduced to about ¼ cup liquid, about 4 minutes.

Add cream and lemon peel, cook 5 minutes.

Stir in mint and tomato and cook 1 minute. Serve on noodles with Lamb Meatballs (see page 156).

Pasta with Smoked Salmon

Serves 2

1 tablespoon butter
1 tomato, diced
½ cup heavy cream
4 ounces smoked salmon
¼ teaspoon black pepper
12 ounces spinach fettucini, cooked
1 teaspoon minced parsley

Heat wok and add the butter. When the butter is melted, add the tomato. Toss, then add the cream. Cook until the sauce thickens slightly. Add salmon, cooking just enough to warm the salmon. Season with pepper. Add fettucini and toss. Garnish with parsley.

Winter Vegetarian Curry

Serves 3

½ cup tomato puree
¼ cup water
½ cup chopped onion
3 tablespoons curry powder
4 cups firm vegetables*
¾ cup frozen peas
1 cup frozen spinach

Bring tomato puree and water to a boil in wok. Add onion and simmer 2 minutes, then add curry powder and mix. Add firm vegetables to wok and stir to coat. Cover and simmer over medium flame for 8 minutes until vegetables are almost tender. Add peas and spinach, cover, and cook for 2 minutes more. Serve with rice.

*Use broccoli, cauliflower, and carrots cut in bite-size pieces for best results. Shredded cabbage is also a good addition.

Couscous Side Dish

Serves 4 as a side dish

2¼ cups chicken stock
½ teaspoon ground cumin
½ teaspoon ground coriander
½ teaspoon paprika
1½ cups couscous
4 tablespoons oil
¼ cup slivered almonds
¼ cup dried apricots, sliced
1 medium onion, cut in ½-inch dice
1 sweet red pepper cut in ½-inch dice
1 cup canned chickpeas, rinsed in water

Heat stock and spices in wok. After it comes to a boil, pour over couscous in a large bowl. Cover and let stand 5 minutes.

Heat wok and add oil. Sauté almonds over medium-low heat until lightly toasted. Remove with a slotted spoon. Sauté apricots, then remove from wok. Raise heat and stir-fry onion and pepper for 3 minutes. Add cooked onion and pepper to couscous. Stir chickpeas, nuts, and apricots into the couscous and serve.

Mushroom Soup Paprikash

Serves 4

3 tablespoons butter
10 ounces mushrooms, sliced
½ onion, chopped
3 tablespoons flour
2 teaspoons paprika
½ teaspoon dill
2 cups water *or* vegetable stock
1 teaspoon soy sauce
1 cup milk
½ teaspoon salt
1 tablespoon lemon juice
½ cup sour cream (optional)

Melt butter in wok. Add mushrooms and onion and sauté 5 minutes. Add flour and spices and stir. Add 1 cup water or stock and soy sauce. Stir and simmer 3 minutes. Add milk and the rest of the water or stock. Cover and simmer 20 minutes, stirring occasionally. The soup will thicken slightly as it cooks. Add salt and cook 2 minutes. Stir in lemon juice right before serving. Garnish with sour cream.

Noodles and Rice

Noodles are extremely versatile. You can serve simmered dishes such as stews over noodles, and they are great complements to stir-fried dishes such as Clams in Black Bean Sauce (see page 86). When substituting noodles for rice with stir-fried dishes, a touch more moisture may be necessary. Add ¼ cup stock and 1 teaspoon soy sauce to stir-fried dishes that appear too dry after preparation with noodles.

Another interesting variation is to use noodles instead of rice for making fried rice dishes. See instructions for fried rice on page 164 and simply substitute noodles for the rice.

Rice is easy to prepare. When I first learned to make rice as a teenager, I was told not to stir the rice or even to lift the lid. I feared the worst if I peeked. Preparing rice isn't that complicated, as I will show you in this next chapter.

When frying noodles or rice, always use leftovers from the day before. Freshly prepared noodles and rice have a lot of water clinging to their surface and you will need to use a lot more oil when you fry them to prevent them from sticking.

Noodles

Dried wheat pasta is the most common type of noodle, the kind you use in Italian dishes. Oriental wheat pasta is slightly pasty, but meatier than Italian spaghetti or linguini. Italian pasta is a fine substitute, though.

Oriental egg noodles are similar to the Western variety. Buy the very thin egg noodles. They are available dried or fresh.

Rice flour noodles are white, thin, long, and transparent. They are often deep-fried as a garnish or as a bed for a strong-flavored dish. Rice sticks are the noodles used in Pad Thai, a Thai noodle dish.

Bean thread noodles are light, white, and transparent. They are used in spring rolls and fried as garnishes.

For variety, try **soba noodles,** a buckwheat pasta used in Japanese cuisine.

Rice

Most households use **long-grain rice.** Throw out those minute and other shortcut rices. White rice takes twenty minutes to cook and it's worth using unadulterated regular rice. It tastes better. Use long-grain rice for fried rice, short-grain for boiled.

Jasmine is a type of long-grain rice that is grown in Thailand and, as its name suggests, is quite fragrant.

Basmati rice is fragrant, too, with a pleasant nutty flavor; it is also not as starkly white as the other long-grain varieties. Basmati, while mostly available in long-grain, does exist in short-grain as well.

Brown rice takes longer to cook (about 35 minutes).

Arborio rice is an Italian short-grain rice used for risottos (slow-cooked, simmered rice dishes).

Short-grain rice is a bit stickier than long-grain, but I find it to be sweeter and tastier.

Sticky or **sweet rice** should be used for stuffings and some desserts.

Basic Rice

1 cup long-grain rice
1¾ cups of water for cooking (¼ cup more or less, depending on how firm or moist you like your rice)

First the rice should be rinsed: Place the rice in a pot and cover with water. Stir the rice with your hand and then strain through a fine colander. Repeat. The rice is now ready for cooking.

Boiling rice is the most familiar method. Place rinsed rice and fresh water in a pan with a tight-fitting lid. Bring to a boil, reduce heat to low, cover, and simmer 15–20 minutes until all the water is absorbed. The rice will have small steam holes in the surface when done. Give the rice a stir, remove from the heat, and let stand covered for 10 minutes before serving, if desired.*

For short-grain rice, use 1½ cups water for each cup of rice.

Another method for boiling rice is to boil the rice in 4–6 cups of water until tender (the same way you cook noodles), then drain and serve.

If you find you like rice and are serving it often, invest in an electric rice cooker that cooks the rice and then keeps it warm.

Variations:
Sauté rinsed, uncooked rice in 1 tablespoon oil before adding water to the rice and boiling it.

Add 1 teaspoon garlic or ginger to the oil before adding the rice.

*Letting the rice stand for a few minutes allows the last bit of water to be absorbed, providing the rice with a finer, fluffier consistency.

Add ½ teaspoon grated orange or lemon peel, or ½ teaspoon curry powder to the oil before adding the rice.

Use broth or stock instead of water to cook the rice.

Replace ¼ cup of the cooking water with sherry or wine.

Add a few saffron threads to the cooking water.

Add any one or a combination of these vegetables to cooked rice:

½ cup cooked peas
½ cup mushrooms sautéed in sherry
¼ cup sautéed onions, peppers, or chopped spinach
2 tablespoons raisins, fresh chopped basil, or Chinese parsley (cilantro)
Sautéed chopped nuts

Fried Rice

The trick to cooking great fried rice is in the egg. Without the egg it just isn't fried rice. For years before I learned how to cook Chinese food I would fry leftover rice, but it never tasted right. Then I learned about using egg. At the end of cooking all the ingredients for fried rice, including frying the rice, you add a lightly beaten egg and toss. As soon as the egg begins to set, the heat is turned off, and the rice is tossed again, and served. The variations on fried rice are endless. Begin by trying these combinations, but soon you will find that just about any leftover can go into fried rice.

Pork Fried Rice

Serves 4

1 tablespoon sherry
2 tablespoons soy sauce
½ teaspoon sugar
2 eggs
3 cups cooked and cooled rice
6 tablespoons oil
¼ pound lean pork, cut in ½-inch cubes
½ cup peas
2 tablespoons minced scallions
¼ cup water chestnuts, sliced in quarters

Combine sherry, soy sauce, and sugar. Set aside. Lightly beat the eggs and also set aside.

Break up clumps in the cooked rice.

Heat wok and add 3 tablespoons oil. When the oil is hot, add the pork and brown for 2 minutes. Add peas, scallions, and water chestnuts and stir-fry 30 seconds. Remove from the pan.

Reheat wok and add 3 more tablespoons oil. When oil is hot, add rice and stir-fry to heat through, 2–3 minutes. Return pork and vegetables to the wok, and stir to mix. Combine soy mixture with eggs, then add to wok. Stir, and flip to coat. When egg begins to set, remove from the heat.

Beef Fried Rice

Marinade:
1 egg white
1 teaspoon sherry
1 teaspoon soy sauce

½ pound beef, sliced thinly against the grain
1 egg
1 tablespoon finely minced scallions
1½ tablespoons oil
1 red pepper, julienned
1 carrot, julienned
½ cup straw mushrooms
3 cups cooked rice
⅓ cup peas
1 teaspoon cornstarch
1 tablespoon water
1 teaspoon sherry
¼ teaspoon sesame oil

Combine marinade ingredients. Toss with the beef and set aside.

Combine egg and scallion and beat lightly. Heat wok and add ½ tablespoon oil. Swirl oil to coat sides. If after swirling there is any leftover oil, pour it out. Add egg. Allow egg to set for a few moments, then swirl to spread egg out. Keep swirling, spreading egg out to form a thin film of egg on the wok. When egg is set, turn off heat before it becomes dry. The egg will continue to cook a bit after the heat is turned off. Carefully loosen the rim of the sheet of egg. Fold the sheet in quarters and remove from the pan. Slice in ½-×-1½-inch pieces.

Heat wok and add 1 tablespoon oil. Stir-fry pepper and carrot 2 minutes. Add beef and mushrooms and stir-fry 2 minutes. Add rice and peas. Toss and cook until rice is heated. Combine cornstarch and water to make a smooth paste. Add sherry, sesame oil, and cornstarch paste. Add egg strips and stir to coat with sauce.

Pork or Duck and Shrimp Fried Rice

Serves 6

2 tablespoons oil
½ cup shredded red-cooked pork *or* duck (see recipe on page 116 or 114)
½ cup peeled, deveined, and diced shrimp
3 cups cooked rice
¼ cup minced scallions
1 egg, lightly beaten
2 tablespoons soy sauce

Heat the wok, then add oil. Add either pork or duck, and shrimp. Stir-fry 1 minute to cook shrimp. Add rice and scallions and stir-fry to heat rice through. Add egg and soy sauce. Stir to coat and cook egg. When the egg begins to set, the rice is done.

Deep-Fried Rice Flour Sticks or Bean Thread Noodles

Serves 2 as a bed for a stir-fry

This is one of the magical wonders of cooking. Sit the kids on a stool or counter close enough to see, far away enough so they can't touch—and watch their and your eyes open wide as the noodles puff up.

3 cups oil for frying
1 ounce bean thread noodles *or* rice sticks

Heat oil in the wok. Separate strands, then add noodles or sticks to oil. Both will puff up almost immediately. Do not brown. Remove once puffed.

Deep-Fried Noodles—Twice Fried

These are the noodles you find on the table in Chinese restaurants for munching and garnishing soups.

3 cups oil for frying
1 pound wide egg noodles, prepared according to package directions

Heat oil in the wok. Place about 1 cup of noodles in a large strainer. Immerse the strainer in the hot oil for about 1 minute. Remove the noodles from the oil and allow to cool, 5–10 minutes. In the meantime fry the other noodles. By the time you're done with the first frying of the second batch, the first batch will be ready for a second frying.

Check the oil to see that it is still hot. Immerse the strainer in the oil and fry the first batch again until crisp and golden. Repeat the process with the second and third batches.

Spiced Summer Vegetables with Noodles

Serves 4

This is a richly flavored dish that makes use of the vegetable bounty of late summer.

1 tablespoon cornstarch
1 cup water
2½ tablespoons rice wine vinegar
2 tablespoons soy sauce
3 tabelspoons fermented black beans
1½ tablespoons minced fresh ginger
2 tablespoons minced garlic
1 teaspoon red pepper flakes
2–3 tablespoons corn oil
8 ounces mushrooms, quartered
1 pound mixed squash quartered (zucchini and yellow summer squash), halved and sliced thinly
½ pound green beans, cut in 1-inch pieces
1 red pepper, diced
1 large Spanish onion, diced
4 ears of fresh corn, cut from the cob
12 ounces thin spaghetti *or* rice noodles, prepared according to package directions.

Dissolve the cornstarch in the water. Add the vinegar and soy sauce.

Combine the black beans, ginger, garlic, and red pepper flakes in a small bowl.

Heat wok. Add 2 tablespoons oil and swirl to coat the wok. Over medium-high heat, add the black bean mixture. Stir until fragrant, about 1 minute. Add mushrooms and cook 1 minute. If mushrooms stick, then add 1 more tablespoon oil. Add the rest of the vegetables. Cook 3 minutes. Add the cornstarch mixture and raise heat to high. The sauce will thicken and turn glossy in less than a minute. Turn off heat, add noodles, toss and serve.

Fried Noodles with Mushrooms

Serves 2 as an entrée or 4 as a side dish

6–8 dried cloud mushrooms
1 cup bok choy, julienned
1 carrot, sliced thinly
2 teaspoons cornstarch
2 tablespoons soy sauce
1 tablespoon vinegar
1 tablespoon Oyster Sauce (see page 37)
3 tablespoons oil
1 cup fresh button mushrooms, sliced
½ cup fresh straw mushrooms
¼ cup fresh enoki mushrooms
½ 8-ounce can of sliced water chestnuts
½ pound noodles for lo mein (spaghetti or linguini), slightly undercooked
2 tablespoons minced scallions

Soak dried cloud mushrooms in hot water for 1 hour, then strain and reserve liquid. Discard tough stems of mushrooms, then julienne and set aside.

Blanch bok choy and carrot for 5 minutes. Rinse in cold water and set aside.

Combine ½ cup of the mushroom liquid, cornstarch, soy sauce, vinegar, and oyster sauce. Set aside.

Heat oil in wok. Add fresh mushrooms and stir-fry 2 minutes. Add bok choy, carrots, reconstituted dried mushrooms, and water chestnuts. Stir-fry 2 minutes. Add pasta. Stir-fry 1–2 minutes. Add mushroom liquid mixture and stir until sauce thickens, about 2 minutes.

Garnish with scallions.

Szechuan Noodles with Beef

Serves 2

½ pound lean beef, sliced thinly
½ tablespoon cornstarch
2 teaspoons *plus* 3 tablespoons oil
½ pound egg noodles, prepared according to package directions
2 scallions, minced
2 tablespoons rice wine vinegar
1 tablespoon chili oil
1 tablespoon sesame oil
1 teaspoon sugar
1 teaspoon salt
½ teaspoon Szechuan peppercorns, crushed
½ cup coarsely chopped pimiento
½ cup cooked peas

Combine beef and cornstarch.

Heat wok. Add 1 teaspoon oil. When oil is hot, add beef and stir-fry 3 minutes. Remove from wok.

Toss cooked noodles with 1 teaspoon oil to keep them from sticking to each other.

Combine scallions, vinegar, chili oil, sesame oil, sugar, salt, and Szechuan peppercorns for sauce. Heat 3 tablespoons oil in wok. Whisk sauce and add to oil slowly while stirring.

Add beef, pimiento, peas, and noodles to sauce in wok and toss to coat.

Noodles Topped with Sautéed Shrimp

Serves 2 as a light first course

3 cups boiling water
6 ounces fine egg noodles
2 tablespoons oil
2 large shrimp, peeled, deveined, and butterflied
1 teaspoon minced garlic
¼ cup grated carrot
2 scallions, minced
1 tablespoon soy sauce
½ teaspoon sesame oil
½ tablespoon rice wine vinegar
1 cup arugula leaves

Pour boiling water over noodles. Let sit 5 minutes, then strain.

Heat wok, then add 1 tablespoon oil. When oil is hot, add shrimp and stir-fry 2 minutes until shrimp is opaque, then remove.

Add 1 tablespoon oil to wok. When oil is hot, add garlic and carrot. Stir-fry 1 minute, then add noodles and scallions. Stir-fry 2 minutes, then add soy sauce, sesame oil, and vinegar.

Serve noodles on bed of arugula. Top with shrimp.

Fried Rice Noodles with Shrimp and Pork

Serves 2

Sauce:

2 tablespoons oyster sauce
2 tablespoons rice wine vinegar
1 tablespoon sherry
2 tablespoons brown sugar
2 dashes Tabasco sauce

4 cups water
½ pound thin rice stick noodles
4 eggs, (beat 2 eggs in one bowl, 2 in another, and keep separate for use at different times)
3 tablespoons oil
½ cup sliced shallots
4 garlic cloves, thinly sliced
¼ pound pork, diced ½-inch thick
¼ pound shrimp, peeled and diced ½-inch thick
½ cup cucumber, julienned
2 tablespoons toasted sesame seeds
1 lime, cut in narrow wedges

Combine sauce ingredients and set aside.

Boil water and soak noodles in boiling water for 4 minutes, until soft. Drain and rinse with cold water, then transfer to a large bowl. Add 2 of the eggs and toss to coat. Drain noodles and then lay out noodles to dry on waxed paper until their egg coating is set.

Heat wok, add 1 tablespoon oil. When oil is hot, reduce heat slightly and sauté shallots and garlic. Cook 1 minute, then remove with a slotted spoon.

Reheat wok, add 1 tablespoon more of oil. When oil is

hot, stir-fry noodles for less than 1 minute until golden. Remove noodles and lay them on paper towels to drain. Don't worry if the noodles stick together.

Reheat wok. Add 1 tablespoon more of oil. When hot, add pork and shrimp. Stir-fry 1 minute until pork is browned. Add remaining eggs slowly, stirring. Add sauce and simmer until liquid evaporates. Add noodles, stir to blend, and heat through.

Garnish with cucumber, sesame seeds, and lime wedges.

Squid with Noodles

Serves 3

Sauce:

1 teaspoon lemon juice
1 teaspoon minced garlic
4 tablespoons oil
4 tablespoons rice wine vinegar
1 teaspoon dry mustard
1 teaspoon sugar
½ teaspoon sesame oil
¼ teaspoon dried red pepper flakes
¼ teaspoon salt

1 pound cleaned squid, cut in 1-inch rings
½ cup large yellow summer squash, julienned
¼ cup diced pimiento
½ pound very thin spinach noodles, cooked
4 radicchio lettuce leaves, julienned

Combine sauce ingredients.

Heat wok. When wok is hot, add sauce, squid, and summer squash. Stir and simmer until squid is opaque and cooked, about 2 minutes. Add pimiento and stir. Remove from heat and toss with noodles. Garnish with radicchio.

Pork and Shrimp Lo Mein

Serves 4

Sauce:

2 tablespoons soy sauce
2 tablespoons sherry
½ teaspoon sugar

¼ pound shrimp, steamed or sautéed until curled and opaque, then minced
½ cup red-cooked pork, shredded (see page 116)
1 egg
1½ tablespoons oil
1 teaspoon minced ginger
1 teaspoon minced garlic
½ cup shredded Chinese cabbage
¼ cup enoki mushrooms
¼ cup sliced water chestnuts
½ cup bean sprouts
¼ cup minced scallions
1 pound wheat noodles, prepared according to package directions

Combine sauce ingredients. Set aside.

Combine shrimp, pork, and egg. Set aside.

Add oil to hot wok. When the oil is hot, add ginger and garlic. Give them a stir, then add vegetables. Stir-fry 2 minutes. Add noodles, toss, and stir-fry 1 minute. Add shrimp and pork and cook 1 minute to heat through. Add sauce and toss to coat.

Noodle Pancake

Serves 6 as a side dish

½ pound noodles of your choice, prepared according to package directions
1 tablespoon sesame oil
3 tablespoons oil

Toss the noodles in 1 tablespoon sesame oil.

Add oil to hot wok. When the oil is hot, add noodles. Spread the noodles out. When the underside is browned (3–5 minutes), turn the pancake over and brown on the other side.

Duck Noodle Soup

Serves 6

Stock from a red-cooked duck
¼ cup scallions, minced
½ of a red-cooked duck (see page 114), chopped into 1-inch pieces, bone included
8 ounces fine egg noodles, prepared according to package directions, but slightly undercooked

Heat stock in the wok. Add enough water to make 4 cups of liquid. Add scallions and heat to a simmer. Add duck and cook to warm duck, then add noodles. When the noodles are warm, serve.

Summer Wok

You might wonder why I included a special chapter on summer wok cooking. Most of the year we're comfortable cooking in our kitchens, but when summer arrives, we resist the idea of a hot meal. As much as we don't wish to cook, meals of raw food lose their luster quickly, so this isn't a chapter of no-cook cold dishes. Summer wokking is about enjoying the bounty of summer. It is also about applying the Chinese cooking technique of contrast to the temperatures of the foods served. Many of the recipes combine stir-fried or fried foods fresh from the wok served with cold, crisp greens. The sauces have more vinegar or lime juice to give the impression of a salad dressing.

Summer Wok Greens

There are three different ways to present the bed of greens for a summer wok dish.

1. Crisp greens such as cabbage and iceberg lettuce are shredded as thinly as possible to form a light, crisp bed for foods to sit upon. The bed, or cloud, as it's sometimes called, should have a bit of height to give the dish some visual appeal. This technique is often used with foods that are fried or oily, because the oil can drip down through the greens. A dressing that contains very little oil is used to compensate for the oil in the fried food.

2. Whole lettuce leaves can be used as wrappers for fillings as in the Ground Beef Thai Salad on page 187. It is one way to turn any dish into finger food at a picnic, or for a bit of messy fun anywhere. Whole lettuce leaves are also used as bowls for fillings on a plate. I recommend leaves from Bibb or Boston lettuce, the tips of leaf lettuces, and, for a bit of color, some radicchio.

3. Serve your favorite greens torn into bite-size pieces as you would for any salad.

Wok-Fried Shrimp and Scallions on Clouds of Lettuce with Sweet-and-Sour Dressing

Serves 2 as a main course, 4 as an appetizer

This recipe has lots of ingredients and explanation, but if you read it through, you'll see it is really quite simple. The dressing and salad will take only a few minutes to prepare and the results are a very attractive and delicious dish.

Shrimp in this recipe are soaked in milk. Many believe the iodine taste that some shrimp have is minimized by a milk bath.

2 cups iceberg lettuce, shredded
1 tomato, sliced
8 cucumber slices
4 scallions, both ends trimmed off
½ cup milk
⅛ teaspoon soy sauce
⅛ teaspoon Tabasco sauce (or 2 dashes)
16 large shrimp, peeled and deveined

Dressing:

2 tablespoons red wine vinegar
4 teaspoons grape jelly
2 teaspoons soy sauce
2 tablespoons salad oil

1 cup flour
⅛ teaspoon ground ginger
1 teaspoon paprika
2 cups oil

Prepare lettuce, tomato, and cucumber as directed. Place a bed of lettuce in the center of the plate. Arrange tomato and cucumber under the top edge of the lettuce. Set aside.

Cut the ends of the scallions 1 inch up the stem on the white end, then cut it again perpendicular to the first cut to form an x when looking at the end of the scallion. Don't cut all the way through so the scallion remains in one piece. Soak cut end in cold water. Set aside.

Pour milk into a small bowl. Season milk with ⅛ teaspoon soy sauce and Tabasco sauce. Marinate shrimp in milk mixture while preparing the dressing.

Combine vinegar, jelly, soy sauce, and oil in wok. Whisk with a fork over a low flame until jelly dissolves. Pour dressing into a small container and chill.

Drain shrimp and save liquid. Combine flour, ginger, and paprika in a small bowl. Heat oil in wok. Dip shrimp in milk, then flour mixture, then repeat with the same shrimp (double dip) and place in hot (but not smoking) oil over medium heat. Repeat with the remainder of the shrimp. Fry each shrimp 2–3 minutes until golden, and drain on paper towels.

Dip white end of scallions in milk, then flour mixture, and fry for 2 minutes until browning begins. Drain on paper towels.

Arrange shrimp on the bottom edge of the bed of lettuce. Top with scallions. Drizzle dressing over the whole plate and serve.

Variations:
As an hors d'oeuvre—Leave out the cucumber and tomato. Arrange lettuce on a tray. Double the shrimp portion of the recipe. Serve with the dressing as a dipping sauce. Garnish the tray with scallions.

Pasta with Peanut Sauce

Serves 4 as an appetizer

This is the peanut sauce that is served with grilled meats for Thai saté, but it is also the best version I have found for pasta. There are easier blender versions of this sauce,* but I think you'll find this version to be smoother and richer.

I recommend making this sauce a day in advance to allow it to cool. If the sauce is poured hot over pasta, it will be absorbed into the pasta and become sticky. One last warning: This sauce is so good that even if you double or quadruple this recipe, it won't be enough.

1½ tablespoons oil
1 medium onion, minced
4 teaspoons minced garlic
¼ teaspoon salt
1 teaspoon chili paste (if necessary, substitute ½ teaspoon Tabasco sauce plus ½ teaspoon red pepper flakes)
4 tablespoons peanut butter (either smooth or chunky)
2 tablespoons soy sauce
2 tablespoons brown sugar
2 cups water

*The lazy, easy version to make in the blender: Leave out the onion and garlic, use only ½ cup water, and blend.

¾ pound fully cooked linguini
¼ cup julienned cucumber
2 tablespoons minced scallion
1 tablespoon crumbled roasted peanuts

Heat oil in wok. Add onion, garlic, salt, and chili paste. Sauté until onions are soft and translucent. Turn off the heat and add peanut butter, soy sauce, and brown sugar. Stir over low heat. Add water. It will look very soupy. Simmer uncovered over medium heat. Reduce until at least half the water has cooked off. Sauce will thicken as it cools. If too thick, stir in water.

Toss cooled sauce with linguini and garnish with julienned cucumber and scallion and crumbled peanuts.

Pork Salad

Serves 4

Dry Marinade:

2 teaspoons ground coriander
¼ teaspoon salt
½ teaspoon pepper
½ teaspoon cumin
1 tablespoon sugar
¼ teaspoon crushed red pepper
1 pound thinly sliced lean pork

½ tablespoon oil
1 teaspoon minced lemon zest
2 teaspoons chopped garlic
¼ cup minced onion
⅓ cup crushed roasted peanuts
1 tablespoon soy sauce
2 tablespoons lemon juice
1 teaspoon sesame oil
1 cup bean sprouts
½ cup julienned cucumber
1 cup julienned lettuce
2 oranges, peeled and thinly sliced

Combine coriander, salt, pepper, cumin, sugar, and red pepper. Toss with pork and let sit 15 minutes.

Heat oil in wok. Add lemon zest, garlic, and onion. Stir-fry 30 seconds. Add pork and marinade. Stir-fry about 3 minutes until pork is browned. Add peanuts, soy sauce, lemon juice, and sesame oil.

Toss together sprouts, cucumber, and lettuce. Split salad among 4 plates. Place 2–3 orange slices on the side of each plate. Top with pork salad and serve.

Chinese Chicken Salad

Yield: 4 generous lunch servings

This is a dish that I often make to have around when I know I won't be home to cook. After tossing the noodles, chicken, and vegetables in the wok, I place them in a bowl in the refrigerator. I set the sauce and the sesame seeds out on the counter or next to the bowl in the refrigerator. Everyone knows to eat when they want. They fill a bowl with the Chinese Chicken Salad, drizzle on the dressing and sesame seeds. When served in this manner I find I always have leftover dressing. Check the recipe on page 193 in the chapter on leftovers for a recipe that turns the dressing into a stir-fry sauce.

Sauce:
½ cup soy sauce
¼ cup rice wine vinegar
2 tablespoons minced fresh ginger
2 tablespoons minced garlic
¼ teaspoon red pepper flakes
1 tablespoon sugar
1 tablespoon sesame oil

2 boneless chicken breasts, cut in 1-inch-wide strips
3 cups chicken broth
4 cups water
8 ounces rice noodles
1 cucumber, peeled, seeded, halved, and sliced
4 chopped scallions
2 cups julienned napa cabbage
1 carrot, julienned
12 whole Chinese cabbage or lettuce leaves
2 tablespoons black or toasted sesame seeds

Combine sauce ingredients. Set aside. Make a day in advance, if possible.

Steam chicken strips over chicken broth until opaque and just cooked through, about 5 minutes. Remove chicken and set aside. Reserve broth.

Add 4 cups of boiling water to the chicken broth. Bring to a boil and add noodles. Cook noodles 5 minutes until soft. Strain noodles and rinse with cold water. Cut noodles into 4-inch-long pieces.

Toss noodles, cucumber, scallions, napa cabbage, carrot, and chicken in a cooled wok. If serving immediately, toss with the sauce.

Place three lettuce leaves on each of four plates. Top with the tossed mixture and garnish with sesame seeds.

Eggplant and Beef Salad

Serves 2

I like all the recipes in this cookbook, but there are a few that are extra special to me. This is one of those recipes.

½ teaspoon salt
½ pound eggplant, cut in ½-inch cubes
2 tablespoons minced fresh basil
½ tablespoon minced garlic
2 tablespoons vinegar
1 tablespoon Worcestershire sauce
1 teaspoon cornstarch
½ pound beef, cut in 1-inch cubes
4 tablespoons oil
4 cups lightly packed fresh spinach
4–6 whole lettuce leaves
⅓ cup chopped tomato
6 scallions, chopped

Toss salt and eggplant. Let stand for 30 minutes. Rinse salt off the eggplant.

Combine basil, garlic, vinegar, Worcestershire sauce, and cornstarch. Toss with beef. Set aside.

Heat 3 tablespoons oil in wok. Add eggplant. Stir-fry until tender, about 8 minutes. Remove from wok and set aside on paper towels to cool.

Heat remaining 1 tablespoon of oil in wok. Add beef and brown. Save the beef marinade. Remove beef from wok to cool. Add spinach to wok and the beef marinade. Spinach will wilt in about 1 minute. Turn off stove. Toss eggplant, beef, and spinach.

Serve on pale green lettuce leaves. Garnish with chopped tomato and scallion.

Green Beans and Baby Corn with Lemon Dressing and Almonds

Serves 6 as a side dish

Dressing:

½ teaspoon grated lemon peel
¼ teaspoon dry mustard
¼ teaspoon dillweed
1 tablespoon plus 1 teaspoon lemon juice
1 teaspoon soy sauce
¼ teaspoon sugar

1 pound green beans
1½ tablespoons oil
2 tablespoons crumbled almonds
1 sweet red pepper, seeded and sliced in ½-inch-wide strips
1 15-ounce can whole baby corn cobs, rinsed in water and drained

Mix dressing ingredients, except 1 teaspoon lemon juice.

Cut off ends of string beans, then snap beans in half.

Heat wok, add oil. Sauté almonds over a medium heat until lightly browned. Remove almonds with a slotted spoon but leave the oil. Add beans and peppers. Stir-fry 2 minutes. Add corn and dressing. Toss to coat.

Top with almonds, let cool to room temperature. Dribble remaining teaspoon of lemon juice on top, and serve.

Ground Beef Thai Salad

Serves 3 as an appetizer

This dish is a bit odd. The beef marinates in a lot of liquid and the final product is wrapped in lettuce leaves. These Thai tacos are very refreshing because of the cool crunch of the lettuce. The lime-marinated meat acts as a dressing for the lettuce.

Marinade:

1 tablespoon water
2 tablespoons fish sauce
1½ tablespoons lime juice
¼ teaspoon crushed red pepper

½ pound lean ground beef
1 teaspoon oil
1 teaspoon garlic
1 teaspoon cornstarch
2 scallions, minced
12 soft lettuce leaves
1 orange, peeled and sliced in 12 pieces

Combine marinade ingredients. Add beef and blend to absorb marinade. Refrigerate for several hours (or overnight).

Heat wok. When wok is hot, add oil, then garlic. Give it a stir, then add beef. Do not add any liquid that has been released while the beef marinated. Save that liquid and combine it with cornstarch to make a smooth paste. Brown beef, about 2–3 minutes. Add scallions and cornstarch paste. Stir to coat, 1 minute.

Serve on whole lettuce leaves (Boston lettuce or leaf lettuce) with orange slices. Guests roll the lettuce up around the filling.

Variation:
For a neater meal, shred lettuce, top with beef, and eat with a fork.

Bacon, Mussel, Potato, and Corn Stew

Serves 3

This makes a sort of soupy stew that I serve over noodles. It requires both a fork and a spoon to eat.

This dish came about at a summer house. The corn, potatoes, tomatoes, and the mussels were gathered locally and the evening was a bit windy so we wanted something warm to eat. The original version was made with salmon and mussels.

1 cup diced potato
4 slices of bacon
¼ cup minced onion
2 tablespoons wine
½ cup water
1½ pounds mussels
¾ cup corn
2 teaspoons wine vinegar
2 tablespoons cream
8 ounces cooked spinach fettucine
¼ chopped fresh tomato

Blanch the potatoes for 5 minutes in boiling water.

Heat the wok. Fry the bacon in the wok. Remove when cooked and drain on paper towels. Crumble the bacon.

Leave 2 tablespoons bacon fat in the wok. Remove the rest of the bacon fat. Sauté the onions over medium heat until soft. Add wine and water to the wok. Bring to a boil and add the mussels. Poach the mussels until they open, about 2 minutes. Remove the mussels from the wok. Add the corn and potato to the wok. Add the vinegar, then the cream. Simmer, *do not boil,* until the corn and potato are heated through and cooked to desired tenderness.

Remove the mussels from their shells and return them to the wok.

Serve on noodles and garnish with crumbled bacon and tomato.

Leftovers and Mix-and-Match Recipes

Leftovers can be turned into wonderful new dishes. I have a soft spot for leftovers because testing recipes for a cookbook produces more leftovers than you can imagine. It is that recipe testing that first made me see how to make mix-and-match recipes.

The Chinese put everything to use. Many of us are on a budget, so it is important to not let anything go to waste. The trick here is to make leftovers not taste like leftovers. A wonton made from leftovers will never go to waste.

This book contains a core of recipes, but those recipes can be broken down and recombined with other recipes. For instance, if you like the Picadillo Stuffed Cabbage on page 49, use the same picadillo filling for a wonton. The cheese sauce for the Macaroni and Cheese on page 47 goes great with the Corn Fritters on page 139. Make the sauces for the stir-fries, such as Beef with Tomato (page 75) or Oriental Sloppy Joes (page 83) and toss it with leftover noodles, rice, vegetables, or meat. Not every combination will be a work of art, but you may surprise yourself with a few that come close to it.

Pretty soon you won't be waiting for leftovers, you will

be making a stir-fry just so you can serve stir-fry burritos for dinner. As for rice, there are recipes that need leftover rice. Fresh rice is too moist to use for fried rice or rice pudding. Plan ahead by making more rice than you'll need so you can have some left-over.

Not all of the leftover recipes are in this chapter. See steamed recipes such as Leftover Rice Pudding on page 104, Duck and Cabbage Dumplings (page 102), and the suggestions for using leftover noodles on page 161 for more ideas.

The following suggestions for using leftovers will help you create many more versatile recipes.

Leftover stir-fry can be finely minced and used in dumplings, reheated and served in tortillas, and can be added to rice for Fried Rice (page 164).

Leftover dipping sauces can be used as the sauce for a stir-fry or noodles, or can be added to water to make a flavorful steaming or poaching liquid.

Leftover Barbecue Pork (page 155) can replace the beef in the Stove-Top Tamale Pie (page 57).

Leftover fried onions can be chopped and used as a garnish on Barbecue pork.

Leftover noodles can be added to broth to make soup and leftover rice used to make rice pudding.

There is no such thing as a leftover dumpling or potato chip.

The Red-Cooked Duck (page 114), Red-Cooked Pork (page 116), Steamed Whole Chicken (page 94), and Steamed Shrimp (page 94) are often made just for use in other recipes.

Leftover Salad Dressing or Dipping Sauce Stir-Fry

Serves 3

When I make Chinese Chicken Salad (page 183) I often have leftover salad dressing. This recipe was concocted to use the leftovers. Any sauce you make too much of can be used this way.

1½ tablespoons oil
1 teaspoon garlic
4 cups of green leafy vegetables: cabbage, bok choy, kale, Swiss chard, spinach (3 cups spinach = 1 cup vegetable in this recipe)
¼ cup sliced bamboo shoots
¼ cup sliced water chestnuts
2 tablespoons leftover dressing
1 teaspoon cornstarch

Heat wok. Add oil to the hot wok. When the oil is hot, add the garlic. Give the garlic a stir, then add the greens. Stir-fry 2–3 minutes until greens wilt. Add bamboo shoots and water chestnuts. Stir and then push food away from the center of the wok. Mix dressing with cornstarch to form a smooth paste, then add dressing to the wok and toss to coat vegetables.

Stir-Fry Burritos

Tortillas *or* Mu Shu Pancakes (page 74)
Leftover stir-fry

Place leftover stir-fry in tortilla or pancake. Roll up and steam over water in a wok until warm.

Top with a dipping sauce. Try combining:

2 parts plum sauce
1 part Hoisin sauce

Leftovers in Fried Rice

Serves 4–6

2 tablespoons oil
1–1½ cups leftover stir-fry and leftover meat *or* chicken *or* shrimp, minced
2–3 cups leftover rice
¼ cup scallions
1 egg, lightly beaten
2 teaspoons soy sauce

Heat the wok, add oil. When the oil is hot, add the leftover stir-fry and meat, chicken, or shrimp. Stir-fry to heat through, about 1–2 minutes. Add rice and scallions and cook about 2 minutes. Add egg and soy sauce and stir to coat. When the egg begins to set, the rice is done.

Crescent Dough Fritters

1 cup leftover Red-Cooked Pork (page 116) and Duck (page 114)
1 teaspoon plum sauce
½ teaspoon Hoisin sauce
1 package of refrigerator crescent dough, cut to wonton-size squares

Combine leftovers with plum sauce and Hoisin sauce. Fold meat in crescent dough to form triangles.

Heat oil in the wok. Deep-fry fritters in the wok until golden.

Leftover Stir-Fry Salad

Serves 2 as an entrée

1 cup leftover stir-fry
2 cups salad fixings: shredded lettuce and cabbage, sliced cucumber, grated carrot
¼ cup leftover *or* freshly made dressing, such as Sweet and Sour Dressing (page 179) or Chinese Chicken Salad Sauce (page 183)

Combine stir-fry and salad fixings. Toss with dressing.

Sources

If you can't find the ingredients called for in the recipes, here are a few mail-order sources.

Katagiri & Co. Inc.
224 East 59th St.
New York, NY 10022
(212) 755-3566

Oriental Food Market & Cooking School
2801 West Howard St.
Chicago, IL 60645
(312) 274-2826

For a free brochure and price list, send a self-addressed stamped business-size envelope.
They do not accept credit cards.

Spice Merchant
P.O. Box 524
Jackson Hole, WY 83001
(307) 733-7811

Call for a free catalogue.
Accepts American Express, MasterCard, and VISA.

Tsang & Ma Wokery
P.O. Box 294
Belmont, CA 94000
(415) 595-2270

Call for a free catalogue.
Accepts MasterCard, VISA, and COD.
Carries seeds to grow your own Oriental vegetables.

Rafal Spice Co.
2521 Russell St.
Detroit, MI 48207
(313) 259-6373

Call for a free catalogue.
Accepts MasterCard, VISA, and COD.

International Epicure
17 Magret Terrace
Sparta, NJ 07871
(800) 622-3344

Call for a free catalogue.
Accepts VISA.

China Bowl Trading Co.
830 Post Rd. East
Westport, CT 06881
(203) 222-0381

Call for a free catalogue.
Accepts American Express and VISA.

Those that do not accept credit cards will accept personal checks.